Reinventing
You!

Simple Steps
to Transform
Your
body, mind &
spirit

Dana Arcuri

**Reinventing You! Simple Steps to Transform
Your Body, Mind, & Spirit**

**Reinventing You! Simple Steps to Transform
Your Body, Mind, & Spirit**

**Reinventing You! Simple Steps to Transform
Your Body, Mind, & Spirit**

Book design by Christine Dupre
Editing and formatting by Michele Jones of AIW Press

.

DEDICATION

This book is dedicated to all of the brave-hearted women who refuse to let their physical, emotional, and spiritual battles prevent them from being all that God designed them to be. For the shakers and movers who creatively look outside the box as they reinvent themselves in effort to transform their lives. You inspire me, motivate me, and empower me to continue advocating for my own health.

IN LOVING MEMORY

In loving memory of my sweet lab, Samson, who passed away during the editing of this book. Earlier this year, my family and I noticed that he was slowing down in his old age, had labored breathing, and was not as active as he used to be. Yet he always had a joyful spirit within, full of unconditional love, and was a loyal furry friend. We couldn't have asked for a better dispositioned dog.

As I mourn the loss of Samson, I do not know what is harder. Watching him suffer and be in pain was excruciating for me. It ripped my heart apart. Saying goodbye for the last time cuts like a knife. Just knowing that I will never watch him play ball, chase after his squeaky toys, excitedly tear open his gifts on Christmas morning, or have fun popping balloons, deeply hurts me.

Once again, I sense that I'm experiencing a metamorphosis similar to a caterpillar transforming into a butterfly. The loss of my precious lab has reverted me to the chrysalis stage of development, which is a dark season filled with loss, grief, and setbacks. While this is temporary and part of the circle of life, I anticipate brighter days when I will fully emerge like an adult butterfly who expands her wings to soar.

In the midst of mourning Samson, God has powerfully revealed His love to me. He gently reminded me that despite my painful trials and sadness, He is still sovereign. Even when bad things happen, God is still good. He can use negative circumstances and transform them into a positive life-change. Lastly, through transitions of physical, emotional, and spiritual growth, the Lord is always faithful, which brings me comfort and hope.

MEDICAL DISCLAIMER

This book is not intended as a substitute for the medical advice of physicians. It shall not take the place of a medical evaluation, diagnosis, and/or treatment. The contents inside this book is for educational purposes and to build awareness. This information does not constitute medical advice and the accuracy of the information is not guaranteed. Furthermore, individuals are recommended to seek professional medical assistance in the event they are suffering mental health and/or medical conditions. The natural alternatives and recipes in this book have not been evaluated by the Food and Drug Administration. They are not intended to diagnose, treat, cure, or prevent any disease or disorder. The author assumes no responsibility or liability for claims arising from the use of the recipes and natural options contained in this book.

Contents

**Reinventing You! Simple Steps to Transform
Your Body, Mind, & Spirit**

Introduction

"Like a butterfly stuck in a chrysalis, waiting for the perfect moment, I was waiting for the day I could burst forth and fly away and find my home." ~ Emme Rollins

Have you ever had one of those days when you could not get out of bed? You know what I mean...the kind of morning when you wake up exhausted, cranky, and have a crummy attitude? When you peer at yourself in the mirror and are surprised by the frazzled reflection looking back at you? It's almost as if something isn't quite right, except you can't clearly pinpoint what it is.

All you know is that somehow your life hasn't turn out as planned. As you dig deeper, you discover that you may be in desperate need of a do-over. Yes, that's right, you may desire a complete renovation. To clean out the old to make room for the new. Sighing, you question, *"Where do I begin?"*

In order to transform ourselves, we must first become aware of the current condition of every aspect within our lives. Our physical health, our body, our mind, our emotions, and our thoughts as well as our attitudes and condition of our souls. You see, when God created us, He marvelously wove every cell together with our body, emotions, and spirit at the core of our being. He designed us to be whole. To lack nothing. *"Before I started to put you together in your mother, I knew you. Before you were born, I set you apart as holy."* Jeremiah 1:5 (NLV)

Our physical, mental, and spiritual health are interconnected. Yet when one is out of sync, the other areas become unbalanced. Usually, this is when we find ourselves depleted, ill, unhappy, dissatisfied with life, or disconnected from our Heavenly Maker. We can feel as if we are not truly existing because we're so bogged down with daily struggles. Instead of thriving, we are barely surviving.

Sometimes we have to hit rock bottom before we are ready to make positive changes.

After ringing in the New Year, I had one of those days that turned into one of those weeks. Eventually, it became one of those dreaded months. I was stuck in a funk. It was no surprise when I had a complete meltdown. Grabbing a tissue, I dried my tears. As I sat alone in my living room, the weight of the world was upon me. No matter how hard I tried, I couldn't stop crying. It was like a levee broke loose. Wet tears streamed down my face.

A dark cloak of depression had a grip on me for five solid months. It showed up out of nowhere. I was mystified. Fuzzy cobwebs of confusion left me questioning what I should do. Yet I didn't know the answer. Nor did I understand what God had in store for me or why He allowed such heavy despair to consume me. Firmly, I scolded myself, *"You can't let this get the best of you. It's time for a positive distraction."*

In effort to focus on self-care, I forced myself to go outdoors on that gorgeous afternoon. To soak up sunshine with natural vitamin D and spend time alone with God. Carefully, I gathered my journal, pen, sunglasses, and Kindle, along with a cold drink. My yellow lab, Samson, strolled excitedly behind me anticipating fresh air as we headed into our backyard.

Once I settled comfortably onto my lawn chair, I searched my Kindle for my favorite song. Listening to Kari Jobe, I poured out my heart on paper. With pen in hand, I wrote, *"Dear Lord, this year has spun out of control and it's turned my life upside down. Before I can make decisions or adjustments, I'm knocked down again. It's such a fierce battle that I can barely catch my breath or focus. Where are You? Please make Yourself present."*

Reinventing You! Simple Steps to Transform Your Body, Mind, & Spirit

Instead of worrying about my troubles, I felt prompted to write about what I sensed God saying to me and how He was working in my life. Quickly, I wrote whatever came to my mind. Here are the words or phrases that truly spoke to me:

- Transition
- Change
- Pruning
- Emotional healing
- Being still
- Surrendering
- Uprooting by grace
- Perseverance
- Strength
- Dependence on God
- Overcoming spiritual warfare
- Tested faith

A gentle breeze ruffled through my hair. The warm sun felt good on my skin. Being surrounded by nature sure had a calming effect. I was grateful for this little escape. Samson laid beside me on the porch. He enjoyed our time together even though I was busy writing.

With uplifting tunes playing in the background, I noticed a butterfly roamed into our yard. It was black with yellow tips on the edges of its wings. The butterfly gracefully fluttered in front of me as if she didn't have a care in the world. She gently meandered in a place of serenity.

I have been living here for five years, and I never saw a butterfly. This caught my attention. I had a hunch the Lord spoke to me. No, I didn't audibly hear Him, but I think He used the butterfly to reveal Himself in such a dramatic way that I wouldn't doubt it was Him. I don't believe in accidents or coincidences.

Instead, I believe events take place in our daily lives for a grander purpose.

It's not a mere coincidence a beautiful butterfly crossed my path on this exact day at this precise time, nor is it pure luck the butterfly symbolism paralleled my own circumstance. Even more fascinating was the fact that I had been struggling for five months to write my book, *Reinventing You!* A bit ironic because as I wrote about being transformed, I was actually experiencing my own personal transformation similar to a butterfly.

Although I knew butterflies were a symbol of hope and transition, I didn't fully grasp what the Lord revealed to me, until the next morning when I realized He powerfully orchestrated events to unfold in 2015 for a divine purpose. As I laid on my bed doing gentle stretches, it suddenly occurred to me that seeing a butterfly the day before was a sign from God. It was a light bulb moment when the hazy fog that had plagued me with confusion had finally lifted and everything became crystal clear.

Excited by this glimmer of hope, I had an epiphany. My Heavenly Father used a butterfly as tangible evidence to show what He's doing in me and through me. In effort for me to write and complete my book on being transformed, the Lord actively worked behind the scenes to transform me from the inside out.

Purging old baggage. Releasing negative emotions. Removing businesses and people from my life who don't belong there. Healing old relationships. Rethinking religion by opting for intimacy with my heavenly Father, instead of getting tangled up in messy spirituality. Connecting to the right people at the right time. Making positive healthy changes with pure nutrients.

In essence, as I write about being transformed in the body, mind, and spirit, God powerfully transforms me physically, emotionally, and spiritually. It's as if this book could not be complete, until the Lord completes what He started in me.

Reinventing You! Simple Steps to Transform
Your Body, Mind, & Spirit

To shed what's holding me back to reinvent my own self. To bravely release my fears as I embrace my wings and soar!

For me to fully grow into the woman He wants me to be, it requires surrendering, unexpected losses, and major changes. Of course, it's not easy because it can be quite painful. Did I mention that I squirm when there are sudden changes? Although I may initially cringe when forced to change, I am reminded of a verse from Job 1:21 (ESV), which says, *"The Lord gave, and the Lord has taken away; blessed by the name of the Lord."*

You see, God loves each one of us so much that He will not permit us or the things in our lives to remain the same. Although He accepts us just as we are; imperfect people living in a broken world, He cares too deeply to leave us this way because He made us to become like Christ. Similar to the butterfly that was once a caterpillar, the Lord wants to transform our lives from the inside out; physically, emotionally, and spiritually.

When I researched butterflies, I discovered it's a symbol of remarkable change. An impressive process of metamorphosis. Here's a list of the fascinating butterfly symbolism:

- Renewal
- Growth
- Time
- Change
- Soul
- Grace
- Expansion
- Elegance
- Surrender
- Expression
- Transition
- Resurrection

**Reinventing You! Simple Steps to Transform
Your Body, Mind, & Spirit**

- Vulnerability
- Transformation
- Hope
- Joy
- Celebration

In awe, I marvel at how God creatively used a butterfly to reveal His wonderment. When I gaze at the symbolic words, many of them are the same ones that I wrote in my journal. The lesson learned is that Jesus is at work in each of our lives 24/7. He's intimately involved in our lives even when we may not hear Him or sense His presence.

During stagnant times when we are spiritually dry, He is with us. When we slip into a gray funk where depression looms overhead, He has not abandoned us. We may not understand why we must endure hardships, but we can confidently trust God is always right there with us in the dark.

In reality, we go through a metamorphosis like a caterpillar transforming into a butterfly. This takes time and does not happen overnight. Just as a butterfly starts life as a very small, round egg, which then grows into a caterpillar (larva), we must experience the necessary changes in our faith to develop into a mature Christian.

During this second stage of a caterpillar, it requires ravenous eating so they can quickly grow. This is similar to a baby believer who must first learn to crawl before she can learn to walk. The new Christian will need daily nourishment from God's Word to grow her faith. It's a gradual process of learning how to pray, discerning the Lord's voice, and trusting Him enough to walk in obedience.

Much like the caterpillar who transitions into a third phase called a Pupa (Chrysalis), we embark on a new season in our own lives that may be filled with darkness and trials. It may be a time involving growing pains, feeling stuck, vulnerability, broken relationships, loss of income, and sickness. Yet this is when there are moments of miraculous expansion.

The valuable lessons of metamorphosis teaches us that change is good. These supernatural changes can lead to physical, emotional, and spiritual growth. We must shed the old before we can become renewed. We release old patterns. We give up our stubborn will. We let go of bad habits. We give birth to new ideas, activities, attitudes, and perspectives. We enter a season when our ideas and creativity may be shaped, developed, and honed.

After this is accomplished (during the Chrysalis stage), a new foundation is laid. Sometimes it entails sitting still, letting go, not making permanent decisions, and resting in God's grace. Oftentimes, it can require seeing situations in a new light and trusting the Lord has everything under His control even if our lives are spinning out of control.

Following incredible growth is the last stage of an adult butterfly. Just as the adult butterfly only emerges from the cocoon when conditions are right, our entire lives will flourish on a higher level when our conditions are right. This is the majestic force of God's creation—for us to break free from conforming to our world. To become more like Jesus on earth. To release old behaviors, thoughts, and lifestyles. To have new desires, dreams, and a future. Like a butterfly, we have hope that in time we will emerge from our cocoon, transformed.

At the heart of this book, is my own real life experience of being transformed by God. The reason I am so passionate about thriving physically, emotionally, and spiritually is because seven years ago, I reached rock bottom. It's only when I lost my health, my mind, my cognitive function, and watched my faith take a nose dive that I determined something had to change. If I remained debilitated with fibromyalgia and suffering clinical depression, there was no hope.

Sometimes it takes a hellish ordeal, such as my own, to wake you up and fight for your life. To reach a point where you know that for real change to happen it begins with you. Healing is a choice. Living life to the fullest is a choice. Overcoming adversity is a choice.

In 2010, when I was on the brink of life and death, my mom encouraged me to keep battling for a full recovery. She said, *"Dana, you are an overcomer!"* Her positive words were like a bolt of lightning. A shocking jolt to remind me of who I really am from the inside out. It resonated within my spirit. God designed me to rise above my afflictions; not to give up or lose hope. My mom's powerful words of affirmation were exactly what I needed to hear. It confirmed that I'm emotionally stronger than I ever imagined and it gave me courage to carry on.

In an effort to reduce my physical and emotional pain, I sought multiple healing strategies. This is when I learned that my body, mind, and soul are connected as a whole being. When one area improves, it enhances the others. All three are interwoven as one. This is why I felt led to research and practice holistic health. In essence, holistic health treats the person as a whole; physically, mentally, and spiritually.

When I began practicing natural alternatives to reduce my physical ailments, I noticed it helped with my sleep, decreased my anxiety, and promoted clearer thinking. Through daily action steps to eat whole foods, eliminate toxins, and clean up my diet, I started to regain my health. When I wasn't in such horrible pain, it gave me hope that God had a special plan for my life. As each symptom lessened in severity, I was in awe at my amazing transformation.

There are no words that can fully express the freedom

and joy of getting a new lease on life. To no longer be bound by disabling conditions that held my life hostage. It has truly opened up my eyes to clearly see this—my physical, emotional, and spiritual health matter. My health matters and your health matters. Vibrant health is a gift from God that most certainly should be treasured.

The primary purpose of my book is to reach out to women from all walks of life to passionately equip, educate, and empower them to take back control of their lives. To come alongside those who may need encouragement and motivation to keep walking their walk no matter how dark or dreary. To never give up hope on your health, your body, your faith, and most certainly to never give up on yourself.

Yes, it may take time, hard work, and extra resources to get where you dream to be, but you are worth it! You owe it to yourself to invest in what matters most to you. To invest in your health because your future is depending on it. To invest in self-care because you need to nurture yourself in order to thrive. When you take good care of yourself (physically, emotionally, and spiritually), you are able to take better care of your loved ones and meet their needs.

Being transformed will always begin on the inside. Being transformed involves change. These daily changes lead to reinventing yourself. Keep in mind, reinvention is a process. It requires building awareness. Whether you're trying to lose weight, eat healthier, or focusing on spiritual growth, each time a major shift happens in your life, you have to envision who you will become or risk never reaching your full potential. As you deliberately choose to reinvent yourself, you are forging a path to a brighter future to be transformed into a new, improved you!

CHAPTER ONE

Running On Empty

"We must be still before God." ~ F.B. Meyer

Women wear many different hats. Each unique hat requires something from us. It may affect how we interact with others and the choices we make in our daily lives. Each has its own set of expectations along with responsibilities. Our individual hats may reflect who we are and what is dear to our hearts. We may be a daughter, sister, friend, mother, grandmother, career woman, entrepreneur, student, coach, homemaker, or wife. With endless possibilities of how many hats we wear, it's no wonder we may feel frazzled and depleted.

By nature, we are nurturers. We want to serve others. It's our way of showing how much we care. Usually, we give and we give and we give, until we're utterly exhausted. Oftentimes, wearing multiple hats is a juggling act. We can easily get so wrapped up in doing what we believe is right or what we feel obligated to do that our lives become unbalanced.

This is where I was last year...running on empty. On the surface, my life seemed fulfilling, complete, and productive. I had launched my second book and I was a recognized leader in a network marketing company. Wearing many hats, I juggled motherhood with being a wife, sister, daughter, friend, author, speaker, coach, and entrepreneur.

In effort to increase my sales, follow up with customers, lead my team, and build my author platform, I spent many hours, day and night, on social media. It may have begun as harmless. Without being aware, it stole a large chunk of my time and attention. By early fall 2014, I felt consumed. Regardless that on the surface my life seemed fine, I was crumbling bit by bit on the inside. My physical health, emotional well-being, and my faith were unraveling before me. Not to mention, my attitude gradually shifted from being upbeat and positive to feeling spent.

Something was missing in my life. There was no peace. Instead, I had a heaviness in my chest. My fast-paced life was one big blur of running myself ragged. In effort to wear all of my special hats, I was on the go. A shaker and a mover! With a type "A" personality, I believed in taking action and checking off my to do list.

All the while, my spirit nudged me to slow down. The constant pressures, distractions, and demands sucked my life dry. My cup was empty. I needed more of God. I was thirsty for Him. On bended knees, I cried out, *"Jesus, I can't keep up with this stress. There's not enough of me to go around. I'm so tired, but I don't know what to do. Something has to change. Please give me clarity and wisdom."*

I wish that I could say God answered my prayers quickly and everything fell smoothly into place, but that's the furthest from the truth. Rather, it was more like I sensed what He wanted me to do, but I resisted change. What I discovered is that we can wrestle our will for His will, but we can't outrun God.

Sooner or later, He will get our attention. When He prompts us to do something and we don't listen, usually it will present itself repeatedly, until we take heed. In January 2015, when I refused to slow down, it was no surprise when I ended up sick. It's kind of like my body sent me a red alert saying, *"You are out of gas and it's time to refuel. Go to bed and get some rest."*

If only I had listened to God and my body signaling me to stop the chaotic pace, I may have avoided three weeks of enduring an unpleasant virus. Ultimately, I was worn out and headed into a new season with the theme, *Be Still and know that I am God.* Repeatedly, for five solid months, the Lord tucked this scripture onto my heart. "*Be still, and know that I am God! I will be honored by every nation. I will be honored throughout the world.*" Psalm 46:10 (NLT)

When I quietly sought refuge in Christ, another verse that came alive to comfort me was from Exodus 14:14 (NIV), "*The Lord will fight for you; you need only to be still.*" When I checked different versions, I felt the verse from New American Standard Bible was the most eye opening. It spoke volumes to me! The verse said, "*Cease striving and know that I am God; I will be exalted among the nations, I will be exalted in the earth.*" It was a very humbling conviction.

According to Merriam Webster Dictionary, the definition of the word striving means, "*To labor, work, exert oneself, struggle, fight, battle, to devote serious effort or energy, and to struggle in opposition.*" This sincerely resonated within my spirit. For I had been caught up in work, striving to climb the ladder of success, aiming to earn more income, desiring to be recognized, and wanting more. It's great to have dreams and to want more, unless it takes our eyes off of God.

In the busyness of making a living and taking care of our family, we can lose our balance and become burnt out. The end result is being physically exhausted, mentally drained, and spiritually depleted. When we burn the candles at both ends something has to give...our time, our work, our family, our church, our choices, or our priorities. Something or someone will suffer; it's inevitable.

After a revelation from God to stop striving and just be still, He softly whispered, "*Do you not grasp how much I love you? Whether you get promoted or not, whether you write a new book or never craft another word, whether you earn an award for being a top seller or fail miserably, I love you for who you are; not for what you do. You are enough. Simply bask in my presence and draw near to Me."*

In awe, I was blown away! By resting in God, I am refreshed. When I take time to be still and worship the Lord, He quenches my hunger and thirst for Him. Instead of chasing after worldly things, all I need is to rest in Him. By spending time alone with my Heavenly Maker, He fills my cup overflowing.

Have you run yourself ragged? Do you wear many hats that leave you burdened? Are you feeling depleted from the busyness and nonstop demands of life? Today, God wants you to stop striving, to take a deep breath, and to be still. As you soak into His mighty presence and fully rest, let Him fill your cup, until it runs over.

QUESTIONS TO TRANFORM:

1. What are the various hats that you wear on a daily basis?

2. Do you ever feel burdened or exhausted by all the hats you wear?

3. Is there an area in your life where you may be striving to such a high degree that you feel burnt out?

4. Do you need to refresh and be still? If so, in which ways can you commit to nurturing yourself?

"Come to me, all you who are weary and burdened, and I will give you rest. Take my yoke upon you and learn from me, for I am gentle and humble in heart, and you will find rest for your souls. For my yoke is easy and my burden is light." Matthew 11:28 (NIV)

"LORD, You are my portion and my cup of blessing; You hold my future." Psalm 16:5 (HSCB)

"Yes, my soul, find rest in God; my hope comes from him." Psalm 62:5 (NIV)

"...My cup overflows with blessings." Psalm 23:5 (NLT)

CHAPTER TWO

Getting Unstuck

*"I feel that as long as you're honest, you have the opportunity
to grow. It's when you shut down, go into denial, and try to
start hiding things from yourself and others, that's when you
lock in certain behaviors and attitudes that keep you stuck."*
~ Tracy McMillan

When we take a good hard look at the reason we're not living the lives we desire, I believe the heart of the matter is that we're stuck. So many of us are stuck in a rut. We're stuck in stagnant relationships that are far from satisfactory. Stuck in a body that isn't functioning properly. Stuck with crazy emotions that are up one minute, but down the next. We may be a people pleaser, always trying to keep everyone happy. It can be uncomfortable and lead to feelings of frustration or resentment.

Day after day, we become stuck in a vicious cycle, which is no longer serving us. Oftentimes, we're stuck wearing a false mask by being someone we are not. Stuck in anxiety and despair. Stuck in a dead end job. Stuck in old habits, lifestyles, or unproductive patterns that are hindering our pathway to joy, vibrant health, and living life to the fullest.

Trapped, we don't know which way to turn. Getting unstuck seems impossible. Yet we can't imagine carrying on another year in this stuck mode. Overwhelmed. Discontented. Disillusioned. Apathetic. How could we passively go through the motions day after day, year after year, unchanged? There has to more to life than what we're living. So how do we get unstuck?

Five years ago, when I was at my worst physically,

emotionally, and spiritually, I knew something had to change in order for me to get better. After struggling miserably for several years and watching my entire life disintegrate, it became apparent that I needed to try something new. This was a no-brainer. My reality was this: If I continued doing what I had been doing, which wasn't successful then how could I expect positive results?

The biggest step to getting unstuck was getting the heck out of my own way. Seriously, I reached a point in which I forced myself to re-evaluate what mattered most to me. Based on the fact that I became disabled and bedridden, I decided wellness and peace of mind mattered the most to me. It was only after I lost my health when I realized how I wasn't truly living. Not by a long shot! Instead, I was stuck in the muck and my existence was wretched.

On one occasion, I asked myself an important question: *"If this current way of life remains the same, can you accept it?"* Instantly, I thought, *"Absolutely not! I don't want to continue suffering in such agonizing chronic pain."* Taking a slow, deep breath, I determined it was time to stop depending on traditional medicine and relying on doctors to rescue me. I had been there and done that for my entire life. It failed repeatedly and actually dug me further into a black hole.

There were no "magic" pills that would save me. In actuality, the combination of potent prescriptions caused far more harm than good. The long-term consequences and negative side effects did not outweigh the positive. My wake up call to take action happened on October 2, 2010 when I survived a drug overdose in an attempt to commit suicide. It's not that I wanted to die. Rather, my physical, mental, and cognitive health had spiraled out of control that my central nervous system became severely impaired. Therefore, my judgment and reasoning were incapacitated.

Reinventing You! Simple Steps to Transform
Your Body, Mind, & Spirit

Despite feeling powerless to change my pathetic circumstances, I believed God gave me a second chance. I not only needed to get the heck out of my own way, but I needed to get out of His way. Prayerfully, I sought Him for realistic solutions. I cried. I prayed. I journaled. On occasion, I pleaded and begged for His wisdom.

Being stuck serves a spiritual purpose. It's a bountiful harvest for transformation to occur. It tells us that a change is needed. More than any type of outward change, what's really being asked of us is an inner change. It could be a change of heart, change of priorities, a change of beliefs, or even a change of perspective.

When we are stuck in a rut we are being invited to grow and expand. What worked before doesn't work anymore so it's up to us to see where we can surrender and open up to new opportunities. This is when our spiritual development can grow by leaps and bounds. When God maybe calling us to new horizons to enlarge our territories for a greater impact in our world.

Another way to getting unstuck is to be willing to go beyond what is familiar and safe. To let go of doubt. To push past fear. To not let resistance stop us from fully thriving. Even if we are scared, we can try something new. In the midst of uncertainty, there is room for expansion to explore the possibilities of self-improvement.

As for my own challenges with getting unstuck, I had to face my reality. I was diagnosed with an auto-immune disorder, depression, anxiety, and ADHD along with troubling ailments. Truthfully, it didn't look pretty. I was shipwrecked and felt like I was drowning, but once I determined that I wanted to fight for my life, God threw me an anchor of hope. Essentially, my faith and feisty personality gave me the gumption to keep on keeping on. It was the hardest battle I ever overcame, but regaining my health was worth it.

**Reinventing You! Simple Steps to Transform
Your Body, Mind, & Spirit**

Simple Steps to Getting Unstuck:

1. **Recognize If You Are Stuck** – This doesn't mean verbally beating yourself up or making yourself feel badly about your situation. Instead, give yourself grace. Also, build awareness about "why" you are stuck. Is it fear of failure? Perhaps, you don't want to do the work involved with making changes? Is it emotionally or physically painful? Or are you not in a financial position to do what you want to do to get unstuck?

2. **Honesty** – Begin by honestly asking yourself if you've been self-sabotaging or hindering your own progress to get unstuck. No condemnation or criticism. Just be real with your own self on why you are stuck.

3. **Priority** – Get a piece of paper and write down a list of your concerns for yourself; physically, emotionally, and spiritually. After compiling your list, consider which priority needs to have your immediate attention. Place a star beside your top priority and prepare to take action.

4. **Focus** – Take your top priority that has a star beside it and only focus on this one area. By laser focusing on one thing, we can become more productive and successfully resolve issues sooner compared to juggling a dozen concerns at one time.

5. **Smaller Steps** – Take your one area of concern and break it down into smaller steps to make it more manageable. Consider creative ways to simplify the process.

6. **Realistic Goals** – Set realistic goals with a date and specific time frame. For example, if your goal is to lose 40 pounds, avoid high expectations of shedding inches and pounds quickly. Realistically, it took you more than one month to gain it and it will take you time to reach this goal. Remember to write all goals with deadlines on paper to track your progress.

7. **Identify What You Need** – Anticipate and identify what you will need in order to get unstuck. Do you need to ask for help? If so, with who? Do you need someone's emotional support? Will you need to go shopping for healthy food or natural supplements? Spiritually, do you need to connect with other women of faith, find a home church, or spend more time in prayer?

8. **Surrender Control** – Logically, there may be areas within your life in which you desire changes to occur, except you have zero to little control. Perhaps, a loved one has an addiction, your work environment is toxic, or you received a serious medical diagnosis? Keep in mind that you are not responsible for other peoples' behaviors, attitudes, or actions. Also, there will be times when you may need to relinquish all control to God. Sometimes letting go is the kindest act of getting unstuck that can lead you to peace.

9. **Personal Accountability** – In order to get unstuck, you will need to be accountable to yourself. This means that you will take full responsibility for what you do and what you don't do. You will be responsible for your thoughts, attitudes, actions, behaviors, lifestyle, choices you make, and ability to overcome whatever is holding you back. Personal accountability requires mindfulness, acceptance, honesty, and courage.

10. **Consistency** – I love this quote by John C. Maxwell who says, *"You will never change your life until you change something you do daily. The secret of your success is found in your daily routine."* One key to getting unstuck is taking daily action steps and being consistent. Repetition truly does reap sweet rewards. Ultimately, you have to determine that you are worth it.

Although getting unstuck may look differently for each

person, if we make a realistic plan, gain more insight, and persistently move forward, we do have the ability to turn our lives around. With time, patience, and perseverance, we can successfully reinvent ourselves. As we gradually improve our physical, emotional, and spiritual health, it can empower and transform us. No matter how big or small, celebrate each achievement. Relish in how far you have come and that you are victorious!

QUESTIONS TO TRANSFORM:

1. Is there an area within your physical, emotional, or spiritual health in which you feel stuck? If so, how long have you struggled with it?

2. Do you need a new perspective to get unstuck?

3. Are you waiting for something outside of your control to change? Have you prayed about this?

4. What can you change within yourself to make improvements? Would an accountability partner help to spur you onward?

"We break down every thought and proud thing that puts itself up against the wisdom of God. We take hold of every thought and make it obey Christ." 2 Corinthians 10:5 (NLV)

"Your reality won't change until you do a reality check." ~ Valorie Burton

"We are hard pressed on every side, but not crushed; perplexed, but not in despair." 2 Corinthians 4:8 (NIV)

CHAPTER THREE

Faith is Built in the Dark

*"Faith is walking face-first and full-speed into the
dark."* ~ Elizabeth Gilbert

My biggest leap of faith happened in the dark. Alright, I will be honest, it wasn't exactly a giant leap; more like a baby step. The truth is that my faith didn't grow during the good times, happy celebrations, or victories. Rather, my faith was built when I reached the darkest, lowest pit of despair. While my body and mind were ravaged from potent chemicals, auto-immune disorders, and I was plunged into full-blown depression, this is the precise moment when my faith stretched the furthest.

It was November 2010, when a death wish landed me into the hospital on the psychiatric floor. Fear and suicidal urges consumed me. Despite all medical efforts to reduce my anxiety and depression, my mental health went haywire. Due to severe interactions from pharmaceutical drugs, I encountered a paradoxical reaction. This is when the effect of medical treatment, usually medication, has the opposite effect. Instead of experiencing relief, I was slammed with wicked symptoms that took my body and mind hostage.

As far as I was concerned, my life was hopeless. Regardless of my 17 year walk with God, I scarcely held onto a shred of faith. Drowning in a sea of doubt, I questioned if He abandoned me. Why did my prayers go unanswered? Where was God? Mere words couldn't express how low I had to go before reaching rock bottom.

I believe the root of my problem was toxic overload, which directly led to dangerously impact every facet of my life;

physically, emotionally, and spiritually. Unless an individual experiences similar complications with pharmaceutical interactions, it's not something the average person can relate to. People may think they understand. But unless someone endures a similar situation it's difficult for them to perceive the dire implications of mixing psychotropic drugs.

This was my first time admitted into a psych unit. It was a scary experience. Being there filled me with dread, uncertainty, and increased anxiety. Seeking comfort, I brought a book by Joyce Meyer to help reassure myself of the Lord's ability to heal. In the privacy of my room, I began reading, *Battlefield of the Mind.* One sentence jumped off the page and caught my full attention. It said, *"For God has not given us the spirit of fear; but of power and of love, and of a sound mind."* 2 Timothy 1:7 (NKJV)

God provides us a spirit of a *sound mind . . .*

Courageously, I firmly clung to this verse and affirmed Christ would give me a sound mind. As I dug deeper into His Word, I discovered by nature our thoughts aren't God's thoughts, nor our ways are not God's ways. (Isaiah 55:8-9) Silently I prayed, *"Dear Lord, please conform my thoughts and words to be like Yours."*

I wish from that moment forward my health improved, but that wasn't the case. Instead, my physical and mental health continued to spiral out of control to such intensity I was admitted into a psych unit for the second time. By January 2011, it became apparent that another prescription was the root cause of my deadly symptoms. Following a fast and furious taper, the hospital decided to discharge me after only four short days.

Concerned for my well-being, I requested to stay longer, but the hospital staff refused. It greatly upset me that medical professionals neglected to monitor me following my abrupt change in medicine. Trembling in fear, I packed my luggage uncertain of what was ahead of me.

Within 24 hours of being weaned off the drug, Ativan, I experienced horrendous withdrawal symptoms. An unexpected welcome to Ativan hell; when one is utterly consumed in slimy, dreadful darkness where life is viciously sucked out of you. A wretchedness in which hellish symptoms are magnified to the highest level. Brutal torture on earth, which felt like a refiner's fire. A scorching furnace of affliction.

So it was during this furnace of affliction in which my faith was built in a cloak of darkness. When suffering, pain, and panic coursed through my veins. When gloomy days turned into weeks, weeks turned into months, and months turned into years of slowly recovering. There were times in which I had no strength to pray. Yet I trusted Jesus understood my moanings and groanings right smack in the midst of my torment.

The Bible tells us the Holy Spirit understands us in our weaknesses. Even when we can't audibly speak, He knows our prayers. *"And the Holy Spirit helps us in our weakness. For example, we don't know what God wants us to pray for. But the Holy Spirit prays for us with groanings that cannot be expressed in words."* (Romans 8:26 NLT)

Through my own personal experience of growing faith in darkness, I believe that most Christians will agree our faith is stretched, pulled, and expanded beyond measure during calamity, trials, and tribulations. Here's a list of some rock bottom moments when authentic faith is built:

- When your home is foreclosed and you have nowhere to live.
- At the cemetery when you say your last goodbyes to your precious child who lost their life far too soon.
- After your doctor confirms the lump on your breast is cancer.

- As you wrestle to do what's right when temptation lures you onto the wrong path.
- When you're given a pink slip at your dream job and unexpectedly unemployed.
- As you stand in line at the grocery store and must pay your bill using food stamps.
- After your spouse files for divorce and leaves you for another woman.
- While raw emotions and panic paralyze you with fear.
- When your earnest prayers go unanswered.
- After struggling for a lifetime with _____ (drinking, drugs, overeating, gambling, pornography, overspending, infidelity, shoplifting, etc.)

The beauty of adversity is that when we hit bottom, the only way to go is up. Our faith is built in the dark, in the valleys, and during the back-breaking battles in life. We can be certain this is when God shows up to work miracles behind the scenes. During our struggles to reclaim our lives (physically, mentally, and spiritually) when we're blinded by darkness, Jesus gives us hope. His hope is found in 2 Corinthians 4:6 (NIV), which proclaims, *"For God, who said, "Let light shine out of darkness," made his light shine in our hearts to give us the light of the knowledge of God's glory displayed in the face of Christ."*

The great news is that in spite of our times of despair and darkness, it can still be used for the glory of God. Our messes create our beautiful messages. Our pain can be used for God's gain. He can connect us to the right people at the right time to share our own real life trials in effort to draw others to Him. If you're enduring darkness or a sea of uncertainty, may this remind you that God will shine the brightest during your darkest moments. *"I have come into the world as a light, so that no one who believes in me should stay in darkness."* John 12:46 (NIV)

QUESTIONS TO TRANSFORM:

1. Recall a specific time when you experienced your darkest moment. How did God grow your faith during this difficulty?

2. When you faced trials or tribulations, were you able to audibly pray? Did you ask others to pray for you?

3. Do you relate to Romans 8:26 in which there were times when God heard your groanings and He prayed for you?

4. How could your personal journey building your faith in darkness help others?

"Behold, as your life was precious this day in my sight, so may my life be precious in the sight of the Lord, and may he deliver me out of all tribulation." 1 Samuel 26:24 (ESV)

"The light shines in the darkness, and the darkness can never extinguish it." John 1:5 (NLT)

"The Lord is my light and my salvation—whom shall I fear? The Lord is the stronghold of my life—of whom shall I be afraid? When the wicked advance against me to devour me, it is my enemies and my foes who will stumble and fall. Though an army besiege me, my heart will not fear; though war break out against me, even then I will be confident." Psalm 27:1-3 (NIV)

Morning Lemon Detox

Drinking a glass of water mixed with freshly squeezed lemon juice provides a number of benefits for the body as well as the mind. Here are some of the health benefits:

- Promotes a fresh breath
- Increased energy
- Balanced PH levels in your body
- Improved digestive function
- Glowing skin
- Strengthened immune system
- Detoxifies the liver
- Curbs appetite
- Cleanses urinary tract
- Reduced blood sugar levels
- It can improve your emotional well-being

Ingredients:

- 1 (8 ounce) glass of warm filtered water
- 1/2 of freshly squeezed lemon or pure lemon essential oil

Instructions:

- First thing in the morning before you eat breakfast, fill your glass with warm filtered water.
- Squeeze fresh lemon juice or use 1-2 drops of pure lemon essential oil into the warm water.
- Stir and drink!

CHAPTER FOUR

Movin' and Groovin'!

*"Sometimes the smallest step in the right direction ends up
being the biggest step of your life. Tip Toe if you must, but take
a step."* ~ Naeem Callaway

Ever since I was a young girl, I've never liked gym class
or exercise. When God created me, He must have missed the
coordination gene. There was nothing smooth or graceful about
my movements! I was clumsy and had a knack for getting myself
into embarrassing predicaments.

Good grief, I will never forget the time I was a
sophomore in senior high. There were two teams in an obstacle
race during gym. When it was my turn, I had to go over, under,
and through a series of objects. At one point, I had to jump
through hoops and dive over a garbage can before crossing the
finish line. Instead of leaping over the trash can, I managed to
find myself landing inside of it. Yes, that's right, I ended up
inside the garbage can! With all eyes on *me*. Laughing
uncontrollably.

As you can imagine, it was by far the most humiliating
moment for me. Talk about humbling! This is when I decided
that I despised all forms of physical fitness. Of course, as a
slender teen, I was able to eat whatever I wanted, whenever I
wanted, and it never caught up to me, until my 20's when I
needed to get my body movin' and groovin'.

During this stage of life, it became apparent that my
metabolism slowed down. I decided to design a new plan to burn
off my extra pounds. I knew it involved movement, but I wasn't
quite sure of which method to choose. Going to a local gym was

out of the question. No thank you! That meant serious perspiration, which I loathed sweating. In my opinion, it made for a bad hair day.

In effort to get into shape, I decided that exercise needed to be fun. Through the years, I've continued to believe the best work out for me includes upbeat music, plus enjoyable activity without killing myself in the process. Or without landing in trash cans. Ironically, after I gave birth to my second child, women at my church formed a small group where we gathered together to work out to *Leslie Sansone's Walk At Home* video. In the 80's, what started as a few aerobics classes in Leslie's health club grew into the #1 in-home walking program worldwide, with over 18 million DVDs sold.

This was life-changing for me because for the first time, I actually enjoyed exercise. Even when sweat dripped down my face and my fru fru hair went limp. Each week, I dedicated myself to Leslie's *Walk Away the Pounds* (three or four-mile walking aerobics). For me, it was energizing and a game changer. Most importantly, it was a blast working out with other women!

While I realize that not everyone is like me and there's plenty of females who love physical fitness, I trust there's gals who are nodding their heads because they might be uncoordinated or loath exercise. When it comes right down to it, getting fit is work. Hard work. Period.

In order to get real results, it will take time, energy, and consistency. If we don't experience good results, if we despise exercise, if it's too strenuous, takes too much time, is too expensive, or it's boring, we may eventually quit. Joining a gym can be an excellent way to get fit, but it's not the only way. We can enjoy a variety of workouts at home or outdoors. My motto is do whatever works for you! Also, switching up routines can be beneficial as well as keep you stimulated and motivated.

Fun Ideas for Physical Fitness:

- Swimming
- Roller skating
- Gardening
- Hula-hooping
- Dancing
- Biking
- Hiking
- Playing with your kids or grandkids
- Walking outdoors
- Bowling
- Zumba
- Jumping rope
- Going on a treasure hunt
- Walking barefoot on the beach
- Horseback riding
- Aerobic or walking videos
- Jumping on your trampoline
- Playing Frisbee with your dog
- Walking outdoors or inside a mall
- Practicing gentle stretches

Seven Awesome Benefits of Physical Fitness:

1. **Reduce Stress** – Had a rough day? One of the emotional perks of exercise is stress relief.

2. **Boost "Happy" Chemicals** – Physical fitness releases the "feel good" endorphins, which can boost happiness and euphoria.

3. **Increase Vitamin D** – Soak up the sunshine with natural vitamin D by enjoying the great outdoors!

4. **Improve Self-Confidence** – When we are physically

fit, we usually feel better about ourselves, which improves our self-esteem and promotes a positive body-image.

5. **Alleviate Anxiety and Depression** – Need to chase away the blues? According to medical research, keeping physically fit can help people feel calmer, sharper, and more content. In addition, it may boost your mood and combat feelings of gloom.

6. **Good Night's Rest** – Tossing and turning at night? Being physically active on a regular basis can enhance sleep. In addition, when our sleep is improved we usually have a better mood with less stress.

7. **Rev Up Energy** – New research suggests that consistent exercise can fight fatigue and boost natural energy levels. If you're feeling sluggish, you may want to skip the java and head outdoors for a brisk walk. Mentally, getting fit can energize you so you can tackle whatever comes your way.

Know Your Physical Limitations:

Before starting physical fitness, it's very important to be aware of your physical limitations. By all means, if you have a heart condition, obesity, arthritis, vertigo, diabetes, high blood pressure, or any form of injuries or medical conditions, you may want to first seek medical approval before starting a workout program.

Use common sense when deciding on which form of exercise you will practice. For example, I have a long medical history of back problems along with fibromyalgia. Therefore, I must avoid strenuous work outs as well as all types of exercise that may aggravate my conditions, such as sit ups and pushups.

Reinventing You! Simple Steps to Transform Your Body, Mind, & Spirit

If you are new to exercise, begin slowly. Please do not over-exert yourself. Instead, pace yourself and be aware of your body's signals. It's wise to use caution to safely avoid further injury. Over a length of time, you can gradually build up the duration and intensity of your work out. As the saying goes, slow and steady wins the race! It's not always the giant leaps that lead to success, but daily small steps. The goal is to create a fun, yet realistic exercise program that fits *your* unique body and health. Happy movin' and groovin'!

QUESTIONS TO TRANSFORM:

1. Do you enjoy physical fitness? If so, what's your favorite work out? If not, why do you feel this way?

2. What are your current struggles with getting into shape?

3. If exercise were fun and stimulating, do you think you would regularly work out?

4. How can you enhance your physical fitness so it's more enjoyable?

"She is energetic and strong, a hard worker." Proverbs 31:17 (NLT)

"For I can do everything through Christ, who gives me strength." Philippians 4:13 (NLT)

"No discipline is enjoyable while it is happening—it's painful! But afterward there will be a peaceful harvest of right living for those who are trained in this way. So take a new grip with your tired hands and strengthen your weak knees. Mark out a straight path for your feet so that those who are weak and lame will not fall but become strong." Hebrews 12:11-13 (NLT)

CHAPTER FIVE

Let's Be Real

*"Share your weaknesses. Share your hard moments. Share your
real side. It'll either scare away every fake person in your life
or it will inspire them to finally let go of that mirage called
"perfection," which will open the doors to the most important
relationships you'll ever be a part of."* ~ Dan Pearce

The one golden nugget that I learned in life is when we
gather together to support each other through our good and bad
times, we discover we're not alone. The truth is that no matter
how brave we want to be, no matter how much we want to be in
control, or how we try to focus on the positive even when
darkness plunges us into a pit of despair, it's when people
encourage us to just be ourselves that we can be real. When we
graciously accept another person with their flaws, weaknesses,
and strengths, we graciously empower them to know:

- It's alright to not be perfect.
- Your imperfections and life experiences help others
  relate to you on a deeper level.
- You are not alone.
- Being a woman of faith doesn't mean you have it
  altogether.
- God loves you in spite of your mistakes, weaknesses,
  and sins.

Have you ever gone somewhere in which you sense the
person sitting next to you is wearing a false mask? They have a
pretty smile and go through all of the motions acting as if
everything is fine, yet underneath their designer dress they are

23

slowly crumbling. Perhaps, they have control issues, drink until they are numb, or they're trapped in a rocky marriage where they feel isolated? When they bravely remove their facade to be real, it helps you break the toxic trance you are in to remove your own false mask.

How would our lives dramatically transform if we each became our authentic selves? Would we be more sensitive and compassionate if we truly felt their pain? What if we walked in their shoes for one day, what would it be like? Here is a list of "Christianese" phrases we say to people when they are experiencing tough times or a faith crisis that can actually hurt more than help:

1. *"God never gives us more than we can handle."* Really? So your sister shouldn't feel fearful, overwhelmed, or hopeless when her doctor confirms she has stage four ovarian cancer?

2. *"One day at a time."* Excuse me? Try telling this to the mom who just buried her two-year-old son after a drunk driver stole his life. She's not only struggling to get through each day; she's trying to get through each agonizing minute.

3. *"It was God's will."* When the most devastating loss has happened to you, would you want to hear this? How about after you lost your home to a horrible flood? Or you caught your husband having an affair with your best friend?

4. *"If you have faith than you won't have fear."* I disagree. As for myself, I happen to have a lot of faith and fear simultaneously. Five years ago, when I endured wicked withdrawals from potent chemicals and was hospitalized twice, I was beyond scared. I was having panic attacks and living a real life nightmare. Through

hellish suffering, I begged the Lord to help me regain my health, but I admit there were plenty of times I had doubts in God and my faith.

5. *"You must have little faith or you wouldn't have gone through* _____ (Fill in the blank). This one really burns me up! Where in the Bible does it say that we are exempt from hardship, pain, or losses? Nowhere. Why do Christians feel the need to say this when in reality it only causes the person who is enduring adversity to feel ashamed or condemned? Who are we to accuse someone of lacking faith when only God knows their heart and personal situation?

The truth of the matter is that everyone feels broken, lost, stunned, angry, and grieved at some point in their lives. In reality, most of us wouldn't relate to someone who has a perfect body, perfect marriage, and perfect job with perfect children in their perfect home with a perfect white fence. This sounds more like *Leave It to Beaver*! When we come across people who may lead us to believe their lives are a beautiful fairytale, it usually leaves us feeling badly as if something were wrong with us. This is when we may run for cover and hide behind false masks.

Instead of feeling inferior for not having it altogether, what if we embraced our messy, imperfect lives? What if we went to our workplace, mom's group, church, or family gathering and gave ourselves permission to be transparent? To openly admit we are real women with real issues in which we face real temptations, frustrations, and pain? Let's take it one step further. What if we transparently shared that we have moments when we doubt God, question His purpose for our lives, and find ourselves thinking more about our problems rather than pray?

An author named Mike Yaconelli who was a pastor,

church leader, theologian, and co-founder of *Youth Specialties*, was an incredibly authentic man with a deep desire to love God and people. He sums up our challenges on being real by saying, *"What if genuine faith begins with admitting we will never have our act completely together? Maybe messy disciples are exactly the kind of imperfect people Jesus came to earth for and whose company he actually enjoyed–and still enjoys."*

When we choose authenticity, we no longer need to stress over trying to be someone we are not. Don't let the fear of what others think hold you back from being real. If they ridicule or reject you, they have no business being a part of your life. Surround yourself around those who will appreciate, respect, and encourage you for being who you truly are. Today, release the burden of living up to the world's standards by stepping into your authentic self. Empower yourself by freely walking toward the beautiful, authentic woman that God created you to be.

QUESTIONS TO TRANSFORM:

1. Do you feel as if you must have it altogether? What kind of daily pressure does this add to your life, relationships, and how you feel about yourself?

2. Did you relate to any of the "Christianese" phrases? Perhaps, someone had said something similar to you? If so, how did you respond?

3. Which specific part of your life do you find yourself wearing a false mask?

4. How could you become more authentic in being exactly who you are?

"But he said to me, "My grace is sufficient for you, for my power is made perfect in weakness." Therefore I will boast all the more

gladly of my weaknesses, so that the power of Christ may rest upon me. For the sake of Christ, then, I am content with weaknesses, insults, hardships, persecutions, and calamities. For when I am weak, then I am strong." 2 Corinthians 12:9-10 (ESV)

"*Pleasant words are as a honeycomb, sweet to the soul, and health to the bones.*" Proverbs 16:24 (KJV)

"*Do not lie to one another, seeing that you have put off the old self with its practices and have put on the new self, which is being renewed in knowledge after the image of its creator.*" Colossians 3:9-10 (ESV)

CHAPTER SIX

Hearing God

"God's voice is still and quiet and easily buried under an avalanche of clamour." ~ Charles Stanley

Oftentimes, I've had thought provoking conversations with my friends and family about faith. On one occasion, a close friend of mine openly shared her personal challenges with me. Frustrated, she said, *"How come you can hear God and He will reveal to you the most remarkable revelations, but He's silent with me? When I pray and read my Bible, I never hear from God. He hasn't spoken to me the way He does to you."*

Sincerely, I don't know why our Heavenly Creator will speak to some people, but not to others. It mystifies me that we each yearn to hear His voice and fervently pray for Him to speak to us, yet not everyone will be aware of God talking to them. There are times in which I don't sense God is near and I do not hear Him. It's very frustrating, which leads me to wonder the reasons why we may not hear from the Lord.

Questions to Ponder:

- Are we not sure what we're supposed to hear, such as an audible sound?
- Can our lives be so hectic and noisy that we can't hear His voice?
- Do we disbelieve God will truly speak to us?
- Could we have a hardened, unforgiving heart?
- Are we lacking the fine art of listening?

- Is the Lord silent for a higher purpose, such as testing our faith?
- Can we distinguish between the world's voice, own voice, and the enemy's voice?

For those baffled from not hearing God, I will share one of my experiences relating to this topic. In January 2011, I had been hospitalized for the second time from severe interactions with potent chemicals, which wreaked havoc on my physical body, emotional well-being, and cognitive function. Spiritually, I was drowning in a sea of uncertainty and wondering if God even cared about me. I felt isolated and tormented with horrific withdrawal symptoms worse than heroin. Overwhelmed, I cried out, *"Where are You, Lord?"*

The room was silent. God never spoke to me or at least I never heard Him. A week after my discharge from the hospital, I connected with an author friend on Facebook. She sent me a private message inviting me to join her and women of faith who were collaborating a book venture; *Inspired Women Succeed.* The purpose of the book was to provide encouragement and hope. It demonstrated forty brave-hearted Christian women entrepreneurs who faced unfathomable trials with heroic faith. Initially, I thought, *"No way! I have never written a book."*

Despite my being a passionate writer and having a lifetime dream to become an author, I thought I lacked necessary skills to follow my aspirations. I had no intention of getting involved in a writing assignment, especially during my atrocious trial. My deteriorating health was the main concern, especially my declining cognitive function. What choice did I have, except to place writing on the backburner?

Frustrated with my disabling condition, I never shared my embarrassing details with my friend. Instead, I sent her a polite message stating that I didn't have enough time to complete a submission. Upon declining her offer, my friend responded by saying she would give me more time to write. Oh, no, this was not the answer I expected!

Prayerfully, I sought God's will. Although I didn't hear an audible voice, I sensed within my spirit that He wanted me to join this project. It wasn't as if the Lord gave a direct "yes" or "no", but I had a notion that He wanted me to trust Him. When He confirmed that I should contribute as a writer it caught me off guard. Wrestling with the Lord, I insisted, *"No, this is the worst time. I can't do it."*

The truth is that sometimes after we pray, we do hear God, but we don't like His answer. Instead of listening to Him and walking obediently, we resist and rebel. As for myself, I had a perfectly logical excuse to avoid the book venture. As a writer, I felt like a failure and unworthy of being published. Not to mention, I couldn't think straight.

How could I submit my work when I feared that I was losing my mind? In a full-blown power struggle with God, I made my defense by pleading, *"I was discharged from the hospital one week ago. For goodness sakes, I'm in the middle of an acute withdrawal! Lord, how could You ask me to take on a huge task at such a time as this?"*

Once again, I heard God, but I didn't like what He said so I refused to obey. Stubbornly, I resisted His conviction to join the book project. Several days past. I didn't flinch. Not until I discovered I couldn't dodge my Heavenly Father.

Morning through night, He persistently urged me to get to work and start writing. Earnestly, I prayed, *"Lord, I have no idea why You chose this time for me to become a contributing author. You know I'm not well. If this is Your will for my life please give me clarity, energy, and good health. I surrender this book to You. In Jesus name. Amen."*

Apparently, God had more faith in me than I had in myself. Eventually, I trusted His will for me to become a contributing author for *Inspired Women Succeed.* While this made absolutely no logical sense, I believed He knew what He was doing. It was time to follow His lead. Quickly, I wrote to my friend and agreed to join her project. Filled with apprehension and excitement, I began writing.

Deep down, it was scary. What if I fell flat on my face in utter failure? What if I publicly humiliate myself? I feared brain fog, dizziness, nausea, and anxiety. Ativan withdrawals were unpredictable. Yet I wanted with all of my heart to successfully complete what God called me to do. Humbly, I prayed, *"Dear Lord, I can't write without You. Please provide me the exact words, ideas, and scriptures to write. Surround me with Your presence. Help me to finish this work for all of Your glory."*

The first few days were successful with words flowing smoothly. On the third evening, I encountered writer's block. As common as this is for most authors it had me highly agitated. My inspirational flow of creativity came to an abrupt halt. Feeling stuck, I sensed something was wrong. I typed. Deleted. Typed more. Deleted more. My trash can overflowed.

Until that moment, I understood the exact idea's God revealed to me. For unknown reasons, I sensed He changed the direction. It confused me. Self-doubt consumed my mind. Negative thoughts silently badgered, *"You can't do this. You're worthless. How do you think you'll pull this off when you've been severely ill? There's no way you can write this so you may as well quit!"*

Following a trip to a local cafe for my favorite latte, I hoped an extra boost would jump-start my writing. Of course, I planned on another all-nighter. My best writing happened in the evening when my family was asleep. At this point, I needed as much help as I could get, especially since I was unsure how to finish the rest of my story.

After I returned home to finish writing, I sat for several hours feeling perplexed in front of my computer. No matter what I typed I wasn't satisfied. I struggled to write poetic sentences to capture my reader's interest. While the clock softly ticked my heart raced to form a logical sentence. Frustrated, I grew anxious and restless. *"Please help me to write this submission,"* I urged the Lord.

When I quieted myself in prayer, the Holy Spirit gave me a clear revelation. His divine message revealed that my book project was meant to be all about God. Not about me, my health, or obstacles. Not about what I do or how I accomplish it. It wasn't about my skills or talent. Rather, my passion to write is all about *Christ*. He inspires me by providing the words, scriptures, and idea's.

Obediently, I left my tiny office on the second floor and walked downstairs into my kitchen. There were dirty dishes in the sink so I began neatly stacking them inside the dishwasher. Out of nowhere, I began humming a tune, *More Love, More Power*, by Michael W. Smith. Getting wrapped up in the moment, I sang out loud. Wanting to hear the actual song, I walked into my living room, sat down at the desk, and turned on the computer. Once I logged in, I headed to YouTube and listened to this song.

With the lights dimmed, I enjoyed quiet time worshiping the Lord. Over and over, I replayed, *More Love, More Power.* I sang with all of my heart. In the stillness of early dawn, the Holy Spirit stirred in my presence. No, I couldn't visually observe Him or audibly hear Him, but I knew He was right there beside me. It's similar to the wind. We can't see or touch the wind, but we can sense it. Just as the wind may provide a soft breeze on a spring day blowing strands of hair against our face, the Holy Spirit gently moves within our being and speaks to us.

After a spiritually uplifting experience I went back upstairs. Rejuvenated, I felt confident to complete the work God set out before me. When I sat at my desk, automatically the words and thoughts flowed smoothly. It was as if the Lord showered me with His wisdom.

When I finished writing my story at 7:00 AM, I received a second fresh revelation. The reason the Lord specifically called me to this book project was to primarily demonstrate how faithful He is. Realistically, I survived a potent cocktail of chemicals, two hospital admissions, and an acute withdrawal. In this pitiful state, I was at my weakest moment. Despite my suffering and pain, Christ's strength was sufficient.

The valuable lesson learned is God can use anything to speak to us. He can use movies, books, music, dreams, websites, rainbows, injuries, illness, darkness, or even a complete stranger to speak to you and me. For those who want to hear God speak, the first step is to unplug from social media and all of your distractions vying for your attention. In effort to tune into Your Heavenly Maker, you must remain willing and ready to listen even at the most inopportune times, such as when you're in bed trying to sleep.

If you are currently struggling to hear God's voice or questioning if He's speaking to you, try to understand that it may differ from person to person. There isn't always a rhyme or reason to it. God does work in mysterious ways. Usually, when He speaks it's not a loud voice thundering down from heaven in a boisterous way. Instead, it may be a still small voice prompting you to follow specific instructions, a warning, or an idea.

Do you ever wonder if God is speaking to you? How can you be sure that it's the Lord and not yourself, our world, or the enemy? Here are helpful ways to know for certain God's speaking to you:

- It's in alignment with scripture.
- God reveals the same thing to you repeatedly.
- The Lord confirms it with a tangible sign.
- Your gut intuition points to your Heavenly Father.
- The desire grows stronger through time.
- It involves you to step out in faith to trust God.

This week, spend quiet time in prayer to hear what God is saying to you. Then wait upon the Lord in expectancy to see what develops. If it's truly from God, He will repeatedly speak to you about the same topic. In most cases, He will give you peace in which the next step for you is to walk in obedience and do as He instructs. Ultimately, if He's calling you to do something, He will equip you through it.

QUESTIONS TO TRANSFORM:

1. Do you ever struggle to hear God's voice? List one situation in which this happened.

2. Are you distracted when you pray?

3. Can you distinguish between the world's voice, your own voice, and the enemy's voice? If so, how do you know the difference?

4. Have you ever sensed God speaking to you, but you didn't obey because you were not happy with what He said? If so, what did you learn from this experience?

"...If you hear His voice today, do not let your hearts become hard." Hebrews 4:7 (NLV)

"If you do not have wisdom, ask God for it. He is always ready

to give it to you and will never say you are wrong for asking."
James 1:5 (NLV)

*"The one who watches the door opens it for him. The sheep listen
to the voice of the shepherd. He calls his own sheep by name and
he leads them out. When the shepherd walks ahead of them, they
follow him because they know his voice. They will not follow
someone they do not know because they do not know his voice.
They will run away from him."* John 10:3-5 (NLV)

DIY Body Scrub

It doesn't matter if it's summer, winter, spring, or fall, each season is the perfect time to slough off dry, dead skin. Today's pricey beauty scrubs, which contain sugar or salt, can be created inexpensively in the comfort of your home. Making body scrubs is easy and will have your skin glowing beautifully!

Not only will your skin appear smoother, but it will be healthier. Depending on which pure essential oils you choose, your homemade sugar scrub may be invigorating and energizing or relaxing and soothing.

DIY Body Scrub Ingredients:

- 1 cup of white or brown sugar (I prefer raw, organic sugar)
- 1 cup fractionated coconut oil, almond oil, or jojoba oil
- 10-15 drops of essential oils of choice (concentration can vary for each brand)

Directions:

- In a bowl, combine all ingredients.
- Mix well. (The goal for your scrub is to not be too dry or too oily for best results)
- Store sugar scrub in an airtight jar.
- In the shower, use 1 tablespoon as needed. Gently scrub skin with the mixture and rinse well. It will leave your skin feeling silky soft!

Reinventing You! Simple Steps to Transform Your Body, Mind, & Spirit

Energizing and Invigorating Essential Oils:

- Pure Lemon essential oil
- Pure Peppermint essential oil
- Pure Grapefruit essential oil
- Pure Rosemary essential oil
- Pure Eucalyptus essential oil
- Pure Carrot Seed essential oil

Relaxing and Soothing Essential Oils:

- Pure Lavender essential oil
- Pure Frankincense essential oil
- Pure Bergamot essential oil
- Pure Jasmine essential oil
- Pure Juniper Berry essential oil
- Pure Clary Sage essential oil

CHAPTER SEVEN

You Were Made to Thrive

*"You were made to thrive, that is why you always have that
deep sense that there is more. It is the potential that is a part of
your DNA that is longing to be realized. Don't just hope or
dream about living a life of thriving, take action right now and
choose to think thrive, act thrive and live thrive!"* ~ Jeffrey
Allen Love

Oftentimes, we are barely getting by. It's a daily battle to keep our lives running smoothly. Is there enough money in our bank account to cover groceries, utilities, mortgage, and the car payment? How can we get everything accomplished that needs tending to in the amount of time we have? Is there more to life than running from one obligation to the next?

The daily grind starts a mad dash rushing through our morning at a speeding rate; showering, gulping down coffee, checking emails, glimpsing social media, and if we have spare time we quickly eat. For moms with young children, our mornings are more chaotic because we're breaking our necks to get them dressed, lunches packed, and shoo them out the door on time for school. It's a race to beat the clock and stay sane!

Ironically, we do the same thing spiritually. We are merely surviving. We only have enough spiritual energy to make it to Sunday to get refreshed and survive the rest of our busy week. We're fortunate if we find extra time to pray and attend Bible studies or church functions on a regular basis.

There doesn't seem to be enough of us to go around. We're spreading ourselves thin. It's lonely, frustrating, and exhausting. Emotionally, we are drained. We may not understand how it's reached this point. We're just trying to make it through each day.

Somewhere along the shuffle to keep up with our nonstop demands hitting us on every side, we realize we're depleted, worn out, and spiritually dry. Our cup is empty. Our faith may have become stagnant. We can sense God's distance. Did He leave us or did we leave Him? Or could it be that He's been here all along? That He's been patiently waiting for us to stop running this rat race on our own and to call out to Him?

While we're trying to survive physically, emotionally, and spiritually, we're close to collapsing in a heap. Our lives may have lost its balance. We're trying with all our might to hang on. To survive our marriage, family, work, school, or whatever else is just around the bend. Yet God didn't create us to merely get by or to struggle surviving this thing called life. We were made to thrive.

I think Christ knows how much we try to live our lives in the flesh to be self-sufficient and independent. Today, He's reminding us that it wasn't meant to be this way. We were made for so much more. We were designed to depend on Him for all of our needs, including our body, mind, and spirit. The verse in Matthew 11:28-30 (MSG), says, *"Are you tired? Worn out? Burned out on religion? Come to me. Get away with me and you'll recover your life. I'll show you how to take a real rest. Walk with me and work with me—watch how I do it. Learn the unforced rhythms of grace. I won't lay anything heavy or ill-fitting on you. Keep company with me and you'll learn to live freely and lightly."*

Your purpose in life is not to be sick and tired. Nor is it to be spiritually burned out. Or mentally depleted. God designed you to thrive. What does this mean? According to vocabulary.com, the definition of thrive means, *"To flourish or*

*grow vigorously, and it can be applied to something like a
business or to something or someone's actual health. Plants can
thrive in a greenhouse, and children can thrive if they eat and
exercise. If something is thriving, it's doing well – so well that
you can call it blooming."*

In a nutshell, thriving is being transformed from the
inside out. It's living vibrantly with longevity. Thriving is living
to our fullest potential physically, emotionally, and spiritually.
This life-changing process can take your ordinary state of being
from mediocre to magnificent! Thriving increases the quality of
your life. Here are positive thriving traits:

- Bear fruit
- Increase
- Progress
- Develop
- Blossom
- Advance
- Get ahead
- Radiate
- Flourish
- Grow
- Prosper
- Shine
- Succeed
- Turn out well
- Arrive

When we look to God's Word, it reveals that Jesus came
to our earth to give us life. Not just any life, but an *abundant*
one. (John 10:10 ESV) His promises give us hope that He will
graciously pour out His blessings; one after the other. (John 1:16
NIV) We can take comfort in knowing the Lord is our provider
to meet all of our needs in all things, at all times, having all we

need. (2 Corinthians 9:8 NIV)

Along my pathway to healing from chronic pain and depression, it required me to go beyond prayer to change my negative situation. Rather than feeling stuck or simply wishing I would recover, I created realistic goals to turn my health around for the better. These daily action steps involved cleaning up my diet, eating gluten-free, educating myself about wellness, having professional massage therapy to relax my restricted muscles, using pure essential oils and natural supplements, listening to uplifting music, intimately connecting to Christ, and reducing my stress levels.

Based on my personal experience, I believe God calls each one of us to take responsibility for our health; physically, emotionally, and spiritually. Instead of limiting ourselves by wishing or wanting something to improve, God desires us to step out and do something about it ourselves. While the Lord is gracious, omnipotent, and can perform the impossible, He wants us to take action *before* we see the blessing.

The Bible says faith without works is dead. In James 2:14-17 (ESV), it says, *"What good is it, my brothers, if someone says he has faith but does not have works? Can that faith save him? If a brother or sister is poorly clothed and lacking in daily food, and one of you says to them, "Go in peace, be warmed and filled," without giving them the things needed for the body, what good is that? So also faith by itself, if it does not have works, is dead."*

You see, faith without works (tangible action steps) is dead because the lack of faith reveals an unchanged life. We can talk about wanting change, pray about wanting change, write about wanting change, and dwell on wanting change, but if we refuse to move forward by actually doing something that leads to *real change* than we are not truly being faithful children of God. Our lack of actions speak much louder than words.

Reinventing You! Simple Steps to Transform Your Body, Mind, & Spirit

For example, if you want to lose weight and get into shape, you need to exercise on a regular basis, choose healthier foods, and have a target goal with a deadline. If you don't take time to get fit, eat right, or actively pursue your goals than you may have zero results. Therefore, your lack of action results in no change. Ultimately, you must be willing and ready to do what God calls you to do in order to receive the blessing.

In a way, this is a form of tested faith. It's like our Heavenly Father is waiting in the deep end of the water for us to simply trust Him. He wants us to believe His promises. To stop worrying about our own ability to make things happen and to just take that leap of faith. Imagine standing on a diving board in a twelve-foot pool. You could stand there, shiver in fear, and do nothing. Your life will go unchanged and you could miss your blessings. Or you can close your eyes, trust God, and jump right into His loving arms waiting to shower you with abundant blessings.

Today, consider realistic action steps that you can take to improve your physical, emotional, and spiritual health. Trust God has so much more in store for you beyond your wildest dreams. Start telling yourself out loud that you were created to thrive. Speak it. Believe it. Envision that the best is yet to come!

QUESTIONS TO TRANFORM:

1. What specific area within your life do you believe you are merely surviving?

2. What new changes or strategies could you invite into your life?

3. Where can you take responsibility for your outcome? Are you willing to do the work necessary for real change to occur?

4. Are there action steps that you can practice consistently to enhance your overall health; physically, emotionally, and spiritually?

"I came that they may have life and have it abundantly." John 10:10 (ESV)

"From his abundance we have all received one gracious blessing after another." John 1:16 (NLT)

"And God is able to bless you abundantly, so that in all things at all times, having all you need, you will abound in every good work." 2 Corinthians 9:8 (NIV)

CHAPTER EIGHT

Managing Roller Coaster Emotions

"Faith is the art of holding on to things in spite of your moods and changing circumstances." ~ C.S. Lewis

Picture this. It's mid-afternoon when my day hasn't gone as planned. Instead of blissful creative writing, I dealt with nonstop interruptions. The rainy morning began with my lab, Samson, begging to go outdoors. Of course, it meant he'd need to be wiped off with a towel because when it rains my yard turns muddy and his paws are caked with dirt. As I raced down the steps chasing after Samson, I immediately noticed a trail of cat puke along the staircase. Yuk!

The perfectionist in me must stop what I'm doing to clean up Sabrina's mess on my carpet. After all, it may leave a permanent stain. I grab a handful of paper towels, carpet cleaner, and silently pray it will work its magic. Carefully inspecting the area, I decide it looks alright.

In the meanwhile, Samson's anxiously waiting. Quickly, I wash my hands in the kitchen sink before taking him outdoors. When he's done doing his business, I wipe his filthy paws, and we stroll back into our home where I give him a doggie treat. Suddenly my stomach growls to remind me that I haven't eaten breakfast. Looks like I missed my morning coffee, too.

My caffeine fix becomes a top priority. I justify that it could boost my writing ability to help me focus. Within thirty minutes, I enjoyed a piping hot cup of organic coffee, gulped down my scrambled eggs, and was ready to conquer another day of writing. Sitting at my desk, I started a new chapter when I heard my cell phone buzzing with notifications. Instantly, I'm torn between checking my messages or getting back to work. What if it's an emergency?

So I'm trying hard to not permit distractions to get the best of me, but my ADHD has a field day with extra stimulation. Forcing myself to stay on task, I type a few paragraphs when the mailman loudly knocks on the door. This sets off Samson who goes berserk and prepares for guard dog mode. Basically, he pretends to be a ferocious wolf when truly he's a teddy bear at heart. I open the door to greet the mailman when he hands me a small package along with a stack of envelopes. Samson squeezes past me through the doorway and escapes outside where he decides to not only smell everything in sight, but to trample into every puddle. Yikes!

At this point, I am not a happy camper. Under my breath, I mutter a few choice words, but I'm trying to refrain from losing my cool. Firmly, I scold Samson and coax him to come indoors. Nevertheless, I must clean his dirty paws and dry him, again. Before I get a towel, he tramples his sloppy filth all over my living room carpet.

I suppose everyone has their own breaking point? This was mine; stressed out and aggravated. Yep, I was in the midst of a good old fashion hissy fit when I broke out in a horrible hot flash. Good Lord, I felt like I was on fire! With sweat dripping down my neck, I dashed upstairs to find my chocolate stashed in a secret drawer for moments like this.

You know what I mean. Those afternoon meltdowns that turn into an emotional roller coaster. In the heat of the moment, I'm perspiring and savoring every bite of my delicious dark chocolate when tears erupted. Not just a little sniffle, but a roaring waterfall!

Reinventing You! Simple Steps to Transform Your Body, Mind, & Spirit

When I reach over my nightstand to grab a tissue and blow my nose, my Bible glared back at me. Okay, perhaps I'm exaggerating a bit, but I sensed God put on my heart that He still loves me. When mood swings rear their ugly head and I'm totally out of control, He's my sanctuary of peace. Even in the middle of my chocolate-filled pity parties, hot flashes, and tears, He pours out His grace for me.

Sometimes our moods and circumstances are like a roller coaster. They are up, down, and can take a drastic nose dive! Thankfully, we can buckle up with God's promises that He is always faithful no matter what we're facing, including raw emotions. Whether we have it altogether or we're falling to pieces, His love is steadfast. Though our feelings can change as fast as a bolt of lightning God remains unchangeable. The Bible says in Malachi 3:6 (ESV), *"For I the LORD do not change; therefore you, O children of Jacob, are not consumed."*

As strong and as fluctuating as our emotions may be, God's Word is:

- Truer than anything I feel
- Truer than anything I experience
- Truer than any circumstance I will ever face
- Truer than anything in our world
- The same yesterday, today, and tomorrow
- Unchanging and unshakable

How can we be certain of this? Because heaven and earth will pass away, but God's Word will not. You see, no matter how we feel or what our circumstances may be, we can choose to depend on the Word of God as a firm foundation for our faith. Despite our roller coaster emotions and negative experiences, we can learn to take God at His Word.

Reinventing You! Simple Steps to Transform Your Body, Mind, & Spirit

Taking God at His supreme Word means having unstoppable faith. You listen and obey His Word because you are confident that what He says shall come to pass. It's not based on unreliable emotions that are up and down like a roller coaster. Rather, it is based on trusting the Lord is who He says He is. The Bible reminds us in Psalm 25:10 (NET), *"The LORD always proves faithful and reliable to those who follow the demands of his covenant."*

God designed our body, mind, and spirit as *one*. There is an interconnection between all three. If one part is off-balance the other areas may suffer. In order for us to successfully manage our emotions we need to dig deeper into the root cause. If mood swings are bringing you down or hormones are wreaking havoc in your life, consider how you can take better care of yourself.

Simple Steps to Help You Manage Roller Coaster Emotions:

1. **Rest** – Are you getting adequate sleep? Or are you spending wakeful nights tossing and turning? Perhaps, you have young children waking you up or you are in a season in life that is preventing sound sleep? This may explain why you are irritable, extra sensitive, and moody. According to Gallup polls, *"40% of Americans get less than seven hours sleep. Medical studies have related a lack of sleep to health problems and cognitive impairment."* Some helpful tips to improve your sleep naturally include having a routine where you go to bed at the same time each night, use a fan or white noise machine to mute sounds, turn off your cell phone, use dark blinds, soak in a warm bathtub with pure essential oils to induce relaxation, and avoid all forms of caffeine in the evening. Practice time-outs to quiet your soul.

2. **Spiritually Empty** – Do you spend consistent time

alone with God? Or is your schedule so full that you find too much on your plate? In order to refuel our spirit, we need to set firm boundaries and block out time with Jesus. Through prayer, worship, reading our Bible, and talking to our Heavenly Father one on one, we can soak into His divine power. By doing so, we renew our minds, body, and soul so we can tackle regular stress in our lives. Other ideas to fill your spiritual cup is to connect with like-minded women of faith, attend a women's retreat, or find a prayer partner to lift you up in prayer and to be accountable in your walk with the Lord.

3. **Stuffing Emotions** – As females, it's natural to have various emotions ranging from high to low. In order to master our emotions, we must avoid denying feelings of anger, sadness, fear, etc. While our feelings can be unpleasant at times or catch us by surprise, it's healthy to address them right away, rather than push them aside or stuff them with food. If we ignore, dismiss, or repress our emotions, we may consequently set ourselves up for physical ailments, such as migraines, digestive distress, weight gain, insomnia, or high blood pressure. Two tips for addressing emotions in a healthy way is journaling and/or professional counseling. Both are therapeutic methods to work through negative feelings and to find realistic solutions to improve your coping skills and to learn how to express your emotions in an appropriate manner.

4. **Hormone Madness** – If you have symptoms of fatigue, brain fog, hot flashes, skin issues, weight gain, extra inches around the middle, trouble sleeping, PMS, infertility, endometriosis, PCOS, or other female concerns, you may have a hormonal imbalance. Although blood work can indicate a hormonal

imbalance, the most accurate method is saliva testing. Many naturopathic doctors specialize in holistic treatments without harsh drugs or synthetic hormones. Other natural solutions include pure essential minerals, such as magnesium, calcium, selenium, and iodine. Due to nationwide depleted soils, our foods and beverages are deficient in vital minerals and nutrients. Therefore, our bodies are deficient in vital minerals and nutrients, which may lead to diseases, disorders, or hormonal imbalances. Another way to tackle hormone challenges is natural progesterone cream, which can be found in health food stores, online, and through a natural compounding pharmacy.

5. **Exercise** – Want to manage stress and emotions? Get moving! The top solution to naturally boost your "feel good" neurotransmitter, endorphins, is exercise. Virtually any form of exercise, from aerobics to swimming, can act as a stress reliever. If you're not a fan of physical fitness or if you're out of shape, all it takes is 15 to 30 minutes of some form of exercise to release endorphins. By doing so, it can dramatically improve a person's mood, attitude, and self-confidence. Best news of all, it can promote relaxation, lower depression, and improve sleep. Find what works for you, listen to your favorite music, and get your body in motion today!

6. **Nutrition** – In society, most of us have busy lives with plenty of demands. We juggle a wide range of responsibilities, which leave us less time to focus on healthy nutrition. It's common for our nation to live on fast foods, junk foods, sweets, soda, and coffee. However, if this becomes a regular habit, our physical, emotional, and spiritual health will suffer long-term consequences. Scientific research shows that eating a

clean diet can significantly improve our moods whereas
unhealthy eating can do the opposite. For example, high
blood sugar can lead to irritability, while low blood
sugar can cause feels of anxiety, depression, and
lethargy. The bottom line is the foods and beverages we
consume can make or break our emotions. The primary
mood-busting foods to avoid are sugar, processed
foods, Genetically Modified Organisms (GMO), gluten,
and artificial colors, flavors, and ingredients, such as
artificial sweeteners, particularly Aspartame and
Sucralose. While you may think it's too difficult to eat
healthy or to change your eating habits, I learned four
years ago that if we get back to the basics we can keep
it simple. Start slow and make changes over time. You
can gradually substitute bad foods for good ones. Begin
by educating yourself about clean nutrition. Read
books, blogs, and articles pertaining to healthy living
and nutrition. Join support groups, workshops, or
meetup groups in your local community to gain more
insight. Through education, you will come to a better
understanding of how your diet may help or hinder your
overall health. Next, find exciting new recipes to
experiment. You may fall in love with a good food you
never imagined you would eat. If you cave in during a
hectic weekend by eating an entire pizza, just get back
on track the next day. It's about making positive
changes to manage your emotional health. Don't get
discouraged if you slip up. Consider that day a special
treat and be determined to make better choices in the
future. Here's to a healthier you!

QUESTIONS TO TRANSFORM:

1. Do you have moments when you feel overwhelmed with
   roller coaster emotions? If so, share an example of what

happened and how it influenced your overall day.

2. What coping strategies have you used to help you manage your raw emotions?

3. Have your hormones caused you to experience irritability, brain fog, sadness, or emotional meltdowns?

4. Have you considered how your foods and drinks can impact your moods?

5. What action steps are you willing to try in order to manage your emotions successfully?

"But the fruit of the Spirit is love, joy, peace, patience, kindness, goodness, faithfulness, gentleness, and self-control." Galatians 5:22-23 New English Translation (NET Bible)

"Whoever is slow to anger is better than the mighty, and he who rules his spirit than he who takes a city." Proverbs 16:32 (ESV)

"As pressure and stress bear down on me, I find joy in your commands." Psalm 110:143 (NLT)

"Turn to me and have mercy, for I am alone and in deep distress. My problems go from bad to worse. Oh, save me from them all! Feel my pain and see my trouble. Forgive all my sins. See how many enemies I have and how viciously they hate me! Protect me! Rescue my life from them! Do not let me be disgraced, for in you I take refuge. May integrity and honesty protect me, for I put my hope in you." Psalm 25:16-21 (NLT)

CHAPTER NINE

Invest in Yourself

"Your body is the biggest investment that you will ever have in your life. Don't abuse it." ~ Michael Kenneth

The best investment with the greatest return you can ever make is in yourself. Your health is worth it. *You* are worth it! In order to reach your maximum potential with vibrant health, it requires investing in yourself physically, emotionally, and spiritually. While there are free or affordable methods to consider, oftentimes a financial investment is involved to enrich your body, mind, and soul.

For example, if you want to build your character, strengthen your walk with the Lord, or grow spiritually, you have a multitude of options to choose from, including investing in the following:

- Christian conferences
- Women's retreats
- Christian concerts
- Spiritual seminars
- Bibles, devotionals, and Christ-centered books
- Women of faith groups, associations, and memberships
- Uplifting worship and praise music
- Hiring a Christian life coach
- Becoming a member of a local church

For your physical well-being, you may have even more options to choose from in effort to promote good health. Although each healing path may vary from person to person, some wellness options are:

Reinventing You! Simple Steps to Transform
Your Body, Mind, & Spirit

- Fitness membership
- Purchasing exercise DVDs, weights, and equipment
- Organic and healthy foods
- Natural supplements and wellness products
- Professional massage therapy
- Chiropractic care
- Essential oils and diffusor
- Water filter system for your home
- Non-GMO products and foods
- Health-related books, DVDs, and CDs
- Naturopathic doctor or holistic professionals
- Wellness seminars, workshops, and conferences
- Hiring a wellness coach or fitness trainer
- Visiting a nutritionist

Managing our spiritual and physical health will most definitely enhance our emotional well-being. When we consider strategies to improve our mental health there's limitless free or affordable options ranging from having a positive attitude to verbally saying uplifting affirmations. Here are ideas on how to invest in a sound mind:

- Professional counseling
- Pet therapy
- Expressing yourself through an art class
- Essential oils for balancing emotions
- Herbal and natural supplements for moods
- Professional massage therapy for relaxation and stress reduction
- Acupuncture
- Going on vacation to reduce your stress levels
- Joining a local pool for sunshine and natural vitamin D
- Playing an instrument or taking music lessons

Reinventing You! Simple Steps to Transform Your Body, Mind, & Spirit

- Spa day for facial, manicure, and pedicure
- Pampering makeover and hairstyle
- Gardening
- CDs and DVDs geared for improving emotional health
- Stress management workshops or seminars
- Books to help you manage emotions
- Journaling

Whether we can legitimately afford it or not, I believe our health is worth the investment. We can use every imaginable excuse by saying we don't have enough money or time. However, it truly comes down to our priorities. Is it the lack of funds? Or are we spending elsewhere on items unrelated to health improvements? (Gourmet coffee, fast food, sweets, handbags, fashion, entertainment, pedicures, etc.) In order to pick up something new, we may have to put down something that is taking up too much of our time or resources. What are you willing to sacrifice in order to revamp your wellness?

If our physical, emotional, and spiritual health aren't a priority, will we eventually reap long-term consequences, such as illness, becoming spiritually dry, or struggling with the blues? If we don't take care of ourselves, how can we expect to be at our best? Most importantly, what does the Lord say?

Four ways God motivates us to take better care of our health:

- You are taking good care of your body – His temple (1 Corinthians 6:19-20 NIV)
- It glorifies God (1st Corinthians 10:31 NIV)
- It will increase your total well-being and boost your energy—you'll be better equipped for what God has planned for you (Hebrews 13:21 NIV)
- You will be a good witness for Christ. (Acts 1:8 NIV)

- Investing in your health now can pay dividends for your future. Today, know that you are worth the investment. The state of your physical, emotional, and spiritual health do matter to God. Ask Him to give you wisdom for the best ways to invest in yourself to be transformed from the inside out.

QUESTIONS TO TRANSFORM:

1. Do you believe that your health is worth the investment? If not, why do you feel this way?
2. Which area of your life (body, mind, spirit) are you willing to invest in?
3. What is holding you back from investing in your overall wellness?
4. List a few affordable methods that you are willing to practice in effort to care for your physical, emotional, or spiritual health.

"Do you not know that your bodies are temples of the Holy Spirit, who is in you, whom you have received from God? You are not your own; you were bought at a price. Therefore honor God with your bodies." 1 Corinthians 6:19-20 (NIV)

"So whether you eat or drink or whatever you do, do it all for the glory of God." 1st Corinthians 10:31 (NIV)

"...equip you with everything good for doing his will, and may he work in us what is pleasing to him, through Jesus Christ, to whom be glory for ever and ever. Amen." Hebrews 13:21 (NIV)

"But you will receive power when the Holy Spirit comes on you; and you will be my witnesses in Jerusalem, and in all Judea and Samaria, and to the ends of the earth." Acts 1:8 (NIV)

HEALTHY SMOOTHIE RECIPE

Healthy smoothies are an excellent way to pack tons of beneficial nutrients into a tasty treat that you can enjoy. Whether you're aiming for a filling and flavorful boost of energy, a protein or post-workout shake, or a delicious beverage for a quick meal replacement, the possibilities and combinations are endless.

Consuming the daily recommendations of fruits and vegetables can be challenging, especially for busy women. Blending a couple of servings of each into a smoothie helps to ensure that you are receiving your daily nutritional needs.

Healthy Smoothie Recipe and What You Will Need:

- A blender, juicer, or NutriBullet
- 3/4 cup of spinach or kale
- 5-6 fresh sliced strawberries
- 1 sliced banana
- 3-4 ice cubes
- 6-8 ounces water (another option is almond or coconut milk)

Directions:

- Add each ingredient to your blender.
- Blend on high, until smooth.
- Pour into a glass and enjoy!

Delicious and Healthy Options to Add to Your Smoothie:

- Fresh pumpkin
- Cinnamon
- Protein powder

- 1-3 drops of Peppermint Essential Oil (check brand for safety of internal use)
- Freshly squeezed oranges or orange juice
- Flax seeds
- Dark cocoa powder
- Fresh carrots
- Almond butter
- Sweet potato

CHAPTER TEN

Battling Our Body and Food

*"When we give up dieting, we take back something we were
often too young to know we had given away: our own voice.
Our ability to make decisions about what to eat and when. Our
belief in ourselves. Our right to decide what goes into our
mouths. Unlike the diets that appear monthly in magazines or
the thermal pants that sweat off pounds, unlike a lover or a
friend or a car, your body is reliable. It doesn't go away, get
lost, stolen. If you will listen, it will speak."* ~ Geneen Roth

Are you exhausted by a nonstop battle with your body
and food? Do you want more for your life than feeling stressed
and stuck in a rut from emotional eating? Have you asked God
to help you take control over your cravings, but find yourself
isolated and struggling with a poor body image?

Throughout my own life my weight has fluctuated,
especially once I reached my middle twenties. Following each
childbirth, I encountered tough challenges losing post-
pregnancy pounds. By far, going through early menopause has
given a whole new meaning to battling the bulge. In between
night sweats, mood swings, and adult acne, my self-esteem
reached an all-time low.

You know what I'm talking about...when you can't look
in the mirror because it will send you into tears or a complete
hissy fit. Oftentimes, both! While trying on clothes in the
dressing room you glimpse at yourself in the mirror and a
frumpy lady glares back at you. And let's not forget the
downright bummer when you try to squeeze into your favorite
jeans, but your zipper won't budge. Not even when you lay flat

on your bed and suck in your tummy.

Crappy doodles! There's a floodgate of emotions erupting inside of me because I know how painful it is to yearn for a thinner body, yet yo-yo back and forth on the scale. When your mind tells you, "*I need chocolate ASAP,*" but deep down inside you know it's going to lead to guilt and shame. And added inches to your waistline. All the while, you can't stop blaming yourself for not looking perfect.

Mystified, you try to figure out why you don't have enough willpower to fight off your urges. No matter how many times you dedicate yourself to getting healthy and fit, you find yourself impulsively making poor choices. Real life happens. Disappointments. PMS. Losses. Sickness. Heavy burdens. Conflicts. Mounting stress. (((Sigh))) So you verbally beat yourself up, until you feel horrible. All you want to do is crawl under a rock and hide. Except you can't fit under a rock, which sends more tears rolling down your face in defeat.

Somehow this brings you full circle back to munching on your favorite cookies, greasy fries, and bag of chips. It's sinfully delightful. While you may not want to confront the truth, food is comforting. In the midst of your storm, it can be soothing and calming. When your nerves are frayed, you may seek food for solace. No doubt, sweets and junk food can be a stress reliever.

Until the day after . . .

This is when we wake up bloated, regretful, and angry at ourselves for caving into emotional eating. Why do we do this to ourselves? How do we overcome this vicious cycle of self-loathing in which our weight determines our state of joy, contentment, and significance? Why do we permit front covers of fashion magazines to make us feel unworthy? Most importantly, how come we place a great emphasis on our shape and size by allowing our self-worth to be based on our outer appearance?

What disturbs me is that I fell into this trap last year. The lies of the enemy said, *"You will be happier if you shed inches and pounds."* After I rang in 2014, I had a quest to look the best. Regardless of how many diet plans had failed, I tried every imaginable method to lose weight, including exercise, shakes, smoothies, essential oils, Paleo and vegan diets, portion control, consuming less calories, fat-free foods, and a dozen different wellness products geared for balancing metabolism. Oh, and let's not forget begging God to answer my prayers.

In the spring, I began using diet supplements that actually started working. Within five months, I successfully dropped three jean sizes, which was unexpected since everything else had failed. On the outer surface, I may have looked as if I were on top of the world, but the truth is that there's no magic number to bring authentic joy. It's a misconception in our world and the enemy's lie. Satan wants women to believe that all we need to do is lose _____ pounds (fill in the blank) to be happy.

Subconsciously, we want to be beautiful, sexy, and loved. We desire for others to accept us, want to be around us, and admire our appearance. We want to be more than the gal with a great personality. When the New Year rolls around, we make resolutions to get back into shape and eat healthy. For the first few months we may experience progress, but somewhere along the way we encounter stress, disappointments, and uncontrollable situations. Call it crazy, but how many of us fall into this trap year after year?

Yes, I was guilty of thinking that if I were not overweight, I'd be more content. To my shocking surprise, I discovered that being skinny doesn't bring *real* happiness. Even more so, I learned that wearing size four doesn't mean that I'm healthy. Despite my initial weight loss success, I still struggled with chronic pain, digestive issues, and inflammation. What good is being thin if your body hurts allover, you can't get out of bed, and you're disconnected from God?

This is when I decided to focus on my overall health; physically, emotionally, and spiritually, instead of getting caught up with the numbers on the scale. In effort to make realistic changes, I decided to get back to the basics. Not my way, but the Lord's way. Immersing myself into the Bible, I asked, *"Dear Jesus, how can I honor You with my body?"*

Immediately, the verse in 1 Corinthians 10:31 (ESV) jumped out at me. It said, *"So, whether you eat or drink, or whatever you do, do all to the glory of God."* Right on the spot, I was convicted. Nervously, I fidgeted as I processed what this scripture meant. In my analysis, it meant munching on sweets when I was stressed out wasn't bringing glory to God. Also, it helped me realize that I needed to build awareness on my motives. How come I craved chips and chocolate when I was feeling down?

Rather than fill my emotions with food, I believed Christ clearly revealed that I needed to seek *Him* to fill up these empty places inside of me. Instead of running to things of our world to complete me (weight loss, beauty, recognition, relationships, success, acceptance, self-worth), God desired me to only look to *Him.* If I want to bring glory to God, it will require me to take back control of my physical, mental, and spiritual health.

In order to glorify the Prince of Peace, we must first come to peace with our bodies. Self-sabotage must stop. We must line up our thoughts, words, and actions with God's Word. In effort to do this, we may need to release old thought patterns and hurtful experiences that have bound us in chains.

The bottom line is that our real battle is not only with our

body and food, but with our mind. (2 Corinthians 10:3-5 ESV)
On a daily basis, we consciously and unconsciously struggle
with negative messages that we hear, read, and speak. We may
have become desensitized to it and are completely unaware of
how it's destroying our self-confidence and self-worth.

Why women may not love or accept their bodies:

- Negative, cruel criticisms from early childhood to adulthood.
- Distorted views of our world.
- Satan's vicious deceptions and lies.
- Unrealistic standards measured by the media.
- The numbers on our scale, which don't tell the whole story.
- Our own unhealthy ideas and beliefs on outer beauty.
- The myth that thin is in.
- Physical or emotional abuse.
- Sexual violation of our body.
- We were told that we are not pretty or good enough.
- Unreasonable pressures from the opposite sex.
- Learned behaviors and poor eating habits as a child.
- Comparing ourselves to others.
- Being bullied.

A lifetime of baggage is too heavy of a burden for us to
carry. To be emotionally set free, we can surrender it to God.
Isn't it time we release our battle with our body and food? To let
go of our painful past, guilt, and shame? Today, we can be
delivered from bondage. We can be set free to walk in God's
peace, love, and grace.

Finding true peace only comes from one place and that
is Jesus. His supernatural peace gives us full permission to

accept and love the precious body He gifted us with. *"Now may the Lord of peace himself give you peace at all times in every way. The Lord be with you all."* 2 Thessalonians 3:16 (ESV)

Dwelling on our outer appearance will not achieve lasting results. If we place a large emphasis on how we look on the outside, we miss the vital component for vibrant health. Instead of gazing outward, we need to shift our focus inward. On a deeper level, we need to make peace with ourselves. To love the person we see from the inside out. Despite our physical and emotional flaws, to respect our unique, imperfect, beautiful selves.

Today, no matter what the size says on your jeans, actively come to a place of peace, gratitude, and self-confidence. Instead of feeding your emotions, draw closer to God and ask Him to nurture your soul. May the Holy Spirit infiltrate His love, grace, and power into every cell of your being in such a profound way that when you glimpse at yourself in the mirror you see the reflection of Christ in you.

QUESTIONS TO TRANSFORM:

1. Have you battled your body or food? If so, when did this begin?

2. What are your "go to" foods or beverages for comfort when you're stressed?

3. Do you ever eat because you're lonely, angry, frustrated, or hurt?

4. Where are you really going to find freedom? In food? In emotions? How about in faith?

5. What triggers your battle with your body and food?

6. How can you find peace with your own body and food?

Reinventing You! Simple Steps to Transform Your Body, Mind, & Spirit

Are you ready to surrender this to Christ?

"Or do you not know that your body is a temple of the Holy Spirit within you, whom you have from God? You are not your own, for you were bought with a price. So glorify God in your body." 1 Corinthians 6:19-20 (ESV)

"For though we walk in the flesh, we are not waging war according to the flesh. For the weapons of our warfare are not of the flesh but have divine power to destroy strongholds. We destroy arguments and every lofty opinion raised against the knowledge of God, and take every thought captive to obey Christ." 2nd Corinthians 10:3-5 (ESV)

"The Lord will fight for you; you need only to be still." Exodus 14:14 (NIV)

CHAPTER ELEVEN

Be Present in the Moment

"Be present in all things and thankful for all things." ~ Maya Angelou

It's mind-blowing how much more we can accomplish when we no longer have distractions. When we unplug from the Internet and social media in effort to take back control of our lives. Our *real* lives need to be fully lived; seizing each precious moment to make the most of it. The purpose of life is not to watch it pass us by. Instead, it's to relish each breath one heartbeat at time. I love an inspiring quote by Eleanor Roosevelt who said, *"The purpose of life is to live it, to taste experience to the utmost, to reach out eagerly and without fear for newer and richer experience."*

Yes, newer and richer experiences include our dreams, goals, and life-long aspirations. Sadly, I believe our nation is so consumed in running the rat race that we've become oblivious to areas within our lives which are taken hostage with our own permission. Primarily, how we spend our time and energy.

In the spring, my family and I headed out to Best Buy to purchase new phones. Our two-year contract ended and we decided to go with another company. Fortunately, all of my contacts and apps on my old phone were able to successfully transfer over to my new phone. After chatting with the salesperson, I discovered that I had a choice, which became quite liberating. Instead of adding the Facebook messenger app to my new phone, I empowered myself by saying, "*No more distractions!*"

The next morning, after I dropped my daughter off at

work, I decided to experiment with *being present in the moment*. Instead of listening to my favorite radio station or CD, I drove in complete silence. It was freeing! Suddenly, I became more aware of birds chirping outdoors and it brought feelings of joy.

While I was waiting at the red light, I noticed that my cell phone was no longer annoying me by dinging in the background to alert me of messages. Also, there were zero disturbances based on the fact that I never logged into social media. TA DA! I relished my time to myself to fully live in the present moment.

This truly opened up more hours for me to be productive each day. To focus on what really matters; my family, my relationships, my health, my faith, and reaching out to the lost to share the love of Christ. My being productive is extremely beneficial because my mission in life is to share a powerful message to our world who is desperately seeking healing, health, and hope. When I'm living in the present moment, I can have a positive impact on the world around me in which God receives all of the glory.

As I ponder how being present in the moment can enhance my overall life, I come to realize that it may create a significant awareness of the blessings that surround me. Instead of rushing around multi-tasking and feeling stressed out over the demands shouting for my attention, I can simply breathe. In the stillness of the moment, peace may become my best friend. Rather than juggling a zillion tasks at onetime, which doesn't work well for my ADHD, I can allow myself freedom to concentrate on my top priorities. Even better, when I'm present in the moment it will open up meaningful opportunities to connect to God on a deeper level to be aware of His omnipotent presence. This is life-changing!

**Reinventing You! Simple Steps to Transform
Your Body, Mind, & Spirit**

Eight Tips to Fully Live in the Present Moment:

1. Become more aware of how you are spending your time daily. Build an awareness of what specific areas may need to be reduced or eliminated.

2. Stop multi-tasking. You do not need to be Super Woman or Super Mom.

3. Start a journal or write a list on paper of everything you are juggling, including with your home, work, and volunteer responsibilities. Remember to add your entertainment and how you spend your spare time. Also, if you are transporting your children to and from activities five days per week, write it down. If you're busy chatting with friends or promoting your business on social media, write it down. This way you may determine specifically what you do within a 24 hour period seven days a week and area's that can be draining your quality of life.

4. Consider unplugging from social media and all distractions for at least 1-2 hours per day. If you are seriously stressed out, you may consider more time to replenish. This may open up opportunities for you to become fully present in the moment. It can help you connect to others in "real" life to build stronger relationships in your home and community.

5. Give yourself permission to fully live in the present moment. Trust that it can reduce your stress and distractions, while empowering you to become more productive and live your passionate purpose.

6. Build your awareness through your senses; sight, sound, scent, touch, and taste. Be aware of your surroundings. Listen to the pitter patter of rainfall. Feel the gentle breeze upon your face or the warm sunshine on your skin. Savor the delightful aroma and the taste of your favorite fresh fruit.

7. Be still. Go to a room in your home or a location outdoors where it's quiet and free from distractions. Turn off or mute your computer, cell phone, and Internet. Take a long, deep breath and slowly release it. Allow your body to relax. Another idea is to soak in a warm bathtub using candlelight to create a calming environment.

8. Spend time in prayer with your Heavenly Maker. Once you are fully present in the moment, you may hear His still soft voice. Give thanks for your abundant blessings. Talk to Him like you chat with your good friend. Treasure your solitude and wait in expectation for God to reveal Himself to you. This can dramatically enhance your spiritual life as you deepen your faith.

Choosing to live in the past or the future not only robs you of enjoyment today, it robs you of truly living. The most important moment is right this very second; the present moment. Although we may slip back into involuntarily thinking about our past or worrying about our future, the more time we spend being mindful of the present moment the easier it can be to reconnect to it and fully embrace it.

QUESTIONS TO TRANSFORM:

1. What specific things are the most distracting to you?

2. Do you take time to be present in the moment? If so, how do you do this? If not, what is preventing you from being present in the moment?

3. How much time do you spend on social media? Have you ever examined how many hours daily or weekly that you are actively engaged on social media?

4. If you were not busy with the Internet or social media, how else would you best use your extra time?

5. Which ways can you consistently practice being present
in the moment?

*"Teach us to number our days, that we may gain a heart of
wisdom."* Psalm 90:12 (NIV)

*"Remember not the former things, nor consider the things of old.
Behold, I am doing a new thing; now it springs forth, do you not
perceive it? I will make a way in the wilderness and rivers in the
desert."* Isaiah 43:18-19 (ESV)

*"Be very careful, then, how you live—not as unwise but as wise,
making the most of every opportunity, because the days are evil."*
Ephesians 5:15 (NIV)

CHAPTER TWELVE

Untangling Messy Spirituality

*"Accepting the reality of our broken, flawed lives is the
beginning of spirituality not because the spiritual life will
remove our flaws but because we let go of seeking perfection
and, instead, seek God, the one who is present in the
tangledness of our lives."* ~ Mike Yaconelli

After being a woman of faith for twenty-two years, I
have come to the conclusion that I will never be a perfect
Christian. While God continues to mold me, change me, and
transform my character to be Christ like, on earth I will never
reach perfection. Despite my desire to do what is right and avoid
making mistakes, there are times I will fail miserably. Tempting
moments when my soul cries out to obey, yet my flesh wrestles
with my sinful nature.

The cornerstone of Christian faith is found in Paul's
letters to the Romans. God uses these letters to powerfully save
lost souls (non-Christians and believers) with the universal
problem of sin. One verse that many can relate to, including
myself, is found in Romans 7:14-15 (NLT), which says, *"So the
trouble is not with the law, for it is spiritual and good. The
trouble is with me, for I am all too human, a slave to sin. I don't
really understand myself, for I want to do what is right, but I
don't do it. Instead, I do what I hate."*

How many times have you slipped up and then promised
God that you would never do it, again? Or you tell yourself that
you will not cave into your flesh with _____ (fill in
the blank), but the next thing you know, you're tangled up in the
wrong things that lead to trouble? Perhaps, we're basically good

70

people with the best intentions, yet living on earth is downright hard? Let's face it, pursuing Christ can be messy.

Nine years ago, I reached a defining moment in my journey of faith when I realized how difficult it was to be a Christian. My eighteen-year marriage hit rock bottom. After professional counseling had repeatedly failed and we struggled for countless years without resolution, I separated from my husband, Tony. Walking away wasn't easy. Rather, it was the most difficult, bleakest moment in my life when I felt utterly alone.

During our separation, confusion tormented me. A part of me wanted to get on with a brand new life and leave my troubled marriage behind. Another part of me questioned why I failed at marriage. I wondered where I went wrong and how I could have been a better wife. Simply put, I felt as if I were the biggest loser.

Having division in a marriage impacts the entire family, including the children. My sixteen-year-old son opted to live with his dad, while my two daughters moved out of our home to live with me. Trying to raise my girls by myself and manage big responsibilities as a single parent brought me to my knees. It was my first time to live on my own, which scared me to death and excited me all at once.

My part-time job and child support didn't cover all of our expenses so this increased my daily stress. Enduring loneliness, doubts, and frustration led me to look to our world for fulfillment. After eighteen years of being devoted to my husband, I started dating when our separation became official.

Although my husband and I were still legally married, I planned on filing for divorce. Of course, money was beyond tight. I had no idea how I would cover the huge expense. My girls and I barely got by on food stamps and medical assistance.

We scrimped and became very thrifty. Trying to make ends meet, I sold their gently used clothes and my book collection at resale shops. Generous people in our church gave me grocery store gift cards and treated me to lunch. Being broke was humbling.

At this early stage in my separation, I felt consumed with anger, bitterness, and resentment toward Tony. Behind my tears and fears, I struggled with a low self-esteem, feeling unloved, and unworthy. In the back of my mind, I justified that dating would be alright because we were no longer together. After years of poor communication and not being emotionally or spiritually connected, I felt certain that our marriage would permanently end.

Quite frankly, the dating scene was brutal and extremely disappointing. When I began going out with Christian men, I discovered they were just as imperfect as I was with their own baggage. This harsh reality left me empty, hurt, overwhelmed, lonely, and with a guilty conscience.

Six months later, in my darkest, vilest moment, I confronted my sin. Yes, I was a married woman of faith who had no longer been faithful to her husband. Why wasn't I strong enough to avoid temptation? It was shameful. Yet in the middle of my mess, the Lord still welcomed me with open arms. He poured out His unconditional love to accept me right where I was at; a broken woman of faith who desperately yearned for mercy and forgiveness to be redeemed.

Looking back, I think it was a remarkable act of grace when God not only forgave me by offering redemption, but He graciously united my husband and I back together in which our dead marriage was resurrected to life. Never in a million years did I expect it to happen, nor did I believe it were possible. Regardless of our human nature to sin and make horrible mistakes, our Heavenly Maker washed away our sins to become white as snow. He sovereignly took two broken people with a broken marriage and transformed us from the inside out.

This is what messy spirituality is.

It's not perfect, neat, orderly, consistent, clean, dependable, unblemished, or even acceptable. Instead, our spirituality is complicated, tested, unbalanced, sloppy, chaotic, imperfect, flawed, messy, shattered, constantly changing, unpredictable, and unfinished. The only way we can be complete and whole is through confessing our sins to Jesus Christ who offers us a clean slate. The Bible says, *"Everything that we have - right thinking and right living, a clean slate and a fresh start - comes from God by way of Jesus Christ."* 1st Corinthians 1:30 (MSG)

Although some people who read about my own failings and sin may find themselves harshly judging me, I ask that you do not fall into this trap. Do not think that Christians are exempt from temptations, unwise choices, and sin. The reality is that *no one* is free from sin. Not me, not you, not the person sitting next to you in the pew, nor leaders within our Christian community.

Oftentimes, we tend to put God and religion in a small box with a rigid set of rules. While we desire to be upright Christians and make the best choices in life, we fail. We are human. In the flesh, we can lead messy lives. Yet our Heavenly Father pours out His grace, mercy, and love upon us because *He never intended for us to be flawless or without sin.* If we were made sinless, Jesus would not have been tortured or sacrificed His own life on the cross. Jesus' resurrection proved His victory over sin and death.

From ancient days, Christians have fallen into the evil trap of legalism where they set a system of man-made regulations for achieving salvation and spiritual growth. People who are legalistic believe in and demand a strict adherence to these rules. For those who don't adhere to these precepts are considered outcasts in the church. Usually, the nonverbal message they receive is, *"You are not good enough and you're not welcomed in this holy place."*

Legalism turns away ordinary folks from all walks of life who may desire to know God on a deeper level, yet they feel ashamed and unworthy of His love and grace. Although they may very well be living in sin and making unwise decisions with inappropriate behaviors, I do not condone what they do. However, the Bible makes it clear that Jesus didn't hang out with the religious law-keepers. Instead, He hung out with and welcomed the lawbreakers; prostitutes, drunks, tax collectors, murderers, and sinners. When Jesus was asked by the prideful lawmakers why He ate and drank with sinners, Jesus replied, *"People who are well do not need a doctor. Only those who are sick need a doctor. I have not come to call those who are right with God. I have come to call those who are sinners."* Mark 2:17 (NLV)

In our society, people who may fall into the outcast category can vary from person to person. While the list is endless, it may include those who battle with the following:

- Smoking
- Drinking
- Drugs
- Gambling
- Food Addictions
- Shoplifting
- Profanity
- Adultery
- Separation/Divorce
- Pornography
- Fornication
- Defiling Your Body
- Homosexuality
- Mental Illness
- Abortions
- Witchcraft
- Incarceration

Real people with real life struggles. Real people with temptations. Real people who may believe in Jesus Christ. Real people who desperately pray for God's grace and forgiveness. Real people who may want to do what's right and have good intentions, but they find themselves doing exactly what they despise.

On the flip side, legalism can also include those who may appear fine outwardly by worldly standards, but on the inside they're wrestling with messy spirituality. They doubt their own faith. Oftentimes, they do not trust God or believe what He says. Silently, they question if they pray enough, tithe enough, volunteer enough, read the Bible enough, attend church enough, or do enough for God.

In effort to climb the legalistic ladder, they work as if in their own flesh it would help them receive approval to enter God's kingdom. Author, speaker, and pastor, Mike Yaconelli, addresses this topic in his book, *Messy Spirituality*, by saying, *"The power of the church is not a parade of flawless people, but of a flawless Christ who embraces our flaws. The church is not made up of whole people, rather of the broken people who find wholeness in a Christ who was broken for us."*

Perhaps, you're struggling with something in your past or present that you know is wrong? Or maybe you are worn out from trying so hard to be a "good" Christian? Stop jumping through legalistic hoops or getting stuck in rigid rules. You are enough just as you are. Whether you are good, bad, or downright sinful, you are enough. Regardless if you regularly attend church or never stepped foot in one, your Heavenly Father welcomes you with open arms. Today, if you find yourself tangled in prayers of dedication or breaths of desperation, cling to Christ who will meet you wherever you are at.

QUESTIONS TO TRANSFORM:

1. Have you ever wanted to do what was right, but found

yourself doing what was wrong? If so, what did you learn from this experience?

2. Are you currently struggling from sins you made in the past?

3. Do you feel as if people judge you for your mistakes?

4. Have you ever felt as if you are not good enough? If so, do you believe that you are enough for Christ just as you are today?

5. Have you asked God to forgive you of your sins? If not, are you ready to ask for grace and forgiveness?

"Not a single person on earth is always good and never sins." Ecclesiastes 7:20 (NLT)

"The sinful nature wants to do evil, which is just the opposite of what the Spirit wants. And the Spirit gives us desires that are the opposite of what the sinful nature desires. These two forces are constantly fighting each other, so you are not free to carry out your good intentions." Galatians 5:17 (NLT)

"Not that I have already obtained this or am already perfect, but I press on to make it my own, because Christ Jesus has made me his own. Brothers, I do not consider that I have made it my own. But one thing I do: forgetting what lies behind and straining forward to what lies ahead, I press on toward the goal for the prize of the upward call of God in Christ Jesus. Let those of us who are mature think this way, and if in anything you think otherwise, God will reveal that also to you. Only let us hold true to what we have attained." Philippians 4:12-16 (ESV)

SOOTHING HERBAL TEAS

Herbal teas are a delicious and easy way to increase your fluid intake and receive extra nutrients. I've always been an herbal tea lover and enjoyed a piping hot cup of tea to use for a wide range of physical and emotional health purposes. If you aren't already an avid tea drinker, here are some soothing combinations to try:

- **Chamomile Tea** – Other than black tea, chamomile tea is one of the most popular consumed tea. Chamomile is a natural source of magnesium and is known as a relaxing and soothing herb. With its mildly sedative properties, chamomile tea is excellent for reducing stress and promoting relaxation in the evening.
- **Ginger Tea** – Ginger is commonly used to treat various types of stomach ailments, including a tummy ache, nausea, dizziness, morning sickness, motion sickness, and other digestive issues. Additional health benefits include weight loss because ginger acts as a fat burner and can help you feel full so you reduce your overall caloric intake. Ginger can also help reduce inflammation, relieve achy muscles, and help the body absorb nutrients.
- **Marshmallow Root Tea** – Marshmallow root has been around for centuries, which contains anti-inflammatory properties. Marshmallow leaf and root are used for pain and swelling of the mucous membranes that line the respiratory tract. This tea is very soothing for coughs, colds, the flu, inflammation of the lining of the stomach, ulcers, urinary tract infections, heartburn, and much more.
- **Mullein Leaf Tea** – Mullein, a plant that grows in dry, barren places, has been used for centuries because of its

outstanding medicinal qualities. Its healing properties are found in its roots, leaves, and flowers, which have been effective in treating a variety of health conditions, especially respiratory disorders. Mullein leaf tea is soothing for asthma, bronchitis, sore throats, coughs, and allergies.

- **Pau d' Arco Tea** – This medicinal tea has anti-inflammatory properties. It is native to South America and has been used to treat many health conditions, including pain, arthritis, fever, ulcers, and candida.
- **Raspberry Leaf Tea** – Is highly nutritious and beneficial for women. Raspberry leaf tea can help balance hormones and is good for the skin. It's often consumed during pregnancy as it can be a good source of magnesium, potassium, and B vitamins. Raspberry leaf tea is recommended for women suffering painful menses, endometriosis, PCOS, and infertility.
- **Slippery Elm Tea** – The inner bark of the slippery elm tree holds the main health benefits, including various nutrients, such as calcium, iron, magnesium, manganese, phosphorus, potassium, selenium, zinc, beta-carotene, and vitamins B1, B2, B3, and C. Slippery Elm tea is used as a mucilaginous herb internally to coat and soothe mucous membranes. It's an effective remedy for duodenal ulcers, gastritis, diarrhea, colitis, irritable bowel syndrome, hemorrhoids, heartburn, urinary tract infections, sore throats, and coughs.

CHAPTER THIRTEEN

A Woman's Self-Worth

*"Consider the fact that maybe…just maybe…beauty and worth
aren't found in a makeup bottle, or a salon-fresh hairstyle, or a
fabulous outfit. Maybe our sparkle comes from somewhere
deeper inside, somewhere so pure and authentic and REAL, it
doesn't need gloss or polish or glitter to shine."* ~ Mandy Hale

Do you flip through fashion magazines secretly wishing you looked like those tall, slim, and stunning models? Have you struggled to lose weight only to find yourself devouring another box of chocolate? Do you wonder if you could ever accept or love yourself just as you are? With blemishes, cellulite, or dark bags under your eyes?

For over twenty-five years, I have worked as an expert in the beauty industry pampering women from all walks of life. Through the years, I've had the exciting opportunity to provide makeovers for local and national television, photography, and special occasions. Regardless of age, race, religion, financial status, or origin, 95% of the women had one thing in common; *lack of self-worth.*

From a sales perspective, the average female would go to great lengths to promote outer beauty. No matter how pricey or drastic the measure, they were on a quest to look their best. It's no wonder the beauty and weight loss industry is a booming business. According to The Statistics Portal, *"There venue of the U.S. cosmetic industry is estimated to amount to about 62.46 billion U.S. Dollars in 2016."*

I believe the root of low self-worth is partly due to our nations distorted perception of beauty. Let's be real for a minute, we all need to know and believe we are worthy. That our lives matter and we count. Yet so many times we are beaten down by society telling us that we're not thin enough, young enough, smart enough, pretty enough, or simply not enough! Why do we base our value on distorted worldly views? Isn't it time we empower ourselves to love ourselves and truly embrace our self-worth?

Here's my main concern with self-worth: If we don't feel worthy, we may not take the time, resources, or focus to intentionally care for ourselves. If we feel unworthy, we may unconsciously neglect to nurture our body, mind, and spirit. When we neglect ourselves, whether we're aware of it or not, we can hinder our overall wellness, which can place ourselves in a vulnerable position that can lead to stress, depression, illness, destructive lifestyles, or stale faith.

Let's go one step further by saying that if we feel unworthy, it may limit our aspirations, motivation, productivity, and ability to succeed. Therefore, we can miss out on opportunities to receive higher income, a promotion, furthering our education, or starting our own business because we may not believe we are even worth it. Instead of going after what our heart truly desires, we may habitually settle for second best, third best, or place ourselves on the bottom of the totem pole.

At their very core, most of our struggles are connected to our self-worth. It makes logical sense that some of our biggest battles are a result of a poor self-esteem and unhealthy self-worth. We have relationship issues, fears, failures, stress, financial troubles, anxiety, bullying, hormonal challenges, disappointments, and losses. Our self-worth is based on what we feel, think, and believe about ourselves.

When we look at the big picture, treating ourselves as if we're not worthy may contribute to the dozen excuses that can potentially hold us back from being all God intended for us to be. Satan likes to viciously attack by making us think that we have no worth and God doesn't value us. Of course, the enemy has a sly way of taunting us by suggesting these lies:

- You do not have what it takes to succeed.
- You don't have the spare time to improve your life.
- You are selfish to even consider nurturing yourself.
- Don't bother because it's too much work!
- It will cost too much money.
- Losing weight has failed before so why try?
- Getting healthy and fit will take too much time.
- You're not worth it!
- You don't deserve to be happy or healthy.
- No one else accepts or loves you so how could God?

Today, my precious friend, we must kick the devil's lies to the curb! Many of us fall prey to self-rejection because we think that nobody loves us or accepts us. We may figure that if nobody else does, why should we? When we think that others don't love us, we might feel as if we must not be worth loving. Those who suffered child abuse (physical, emotional, or sexual) or were raised in a dysfunctional home may believe they're unlovable and unimportant. However, it's a dirty rotten lie we've believed for way too long.

It's vital to tune out the lies of the enemy, world, and toxic people who hurt us with condemnation, rejection, or criticism. No matter how many times we've been mistreated, our past does not define us. In order to clearly distinguish what God says about our worth, we need to let go of old patterns. We can bravely say, *"This is not how my story ends."* Repeat that out loud. Today. Tomorrow. Speak it. Believe it. Immerse yourself into verbally speaking blessings and healing over your life.

It's a daily effort in which we must actively pursue. To

gently shed old voices and toxic thoughts screaming inside our head. Like an onion, each layer is peeled away to burst forth healthy beliefs, new attitudes, and acceptance for the beautiful soul we are. Instead of seeking validation through others, go to the *One* who formed you. He made you complete and whole. Before you were conceived, God chose *you*. The Bible confirms this by saying, *"I chose you before I formed you in the womb; I set you apart before you were born. I appointed you a prophet to the nations."* Jeremiah 1:5 (HCSB)

Isn't it time we line up the Lord's Word to redefine our worth? If you struggle with feeling unaccepted and unworthy, I encourage you to learn what God says to reclaim your birthright of how truly valuable you are. The Bible declares, *"Because you are precious in my eyes, and honored, and I love you..."* Isaiah 43:4 (ESV)

As you begin to see yourself through Christ's eyes (someone who's cherished, valuable, and eternally significant) your view of yourself will transform. Eventually, you will start to see yourself, not as rejected, but as worthy, precious, and highly esteemed. Confidently, you can walk forth as a daughter of Christ because your true worth lies within *Him*.

QUESTIONS TO TRANSFORM:

1. Looking back on your childhood, were you treated as worthy? If not, how did this influence you and the way you felt about yourself?

2. In what ways does the media impact your view of your value and importance?

3. What practical steps can you take to fully flourish with a healthy self-worth?

4. If you have children or grandchildren, how can you help

them build their self-worth?

"So that you may live a life worthy of the Lord and please him in every way: bearing fruit in every good work, growing in the knowledge of God." Colossians 1:10 (NIV)

"What is the price of two sparrows-one copper coin? But not a single sparrow can fall to the ground without your Father knowing it. And the very hairs on your head are all numbered. So don't be afraid; you are more valuable to God than a whole flock of sparrows." Matthew 10:20-31 (NLT)

"Because of the Lord's great love we are not consumed, for his compassions never fail." Lamentations 3:22 (NIV)

CHAPTER FOURTEEN

What a Hoot!

*"Laughter heals all wounds, and that's one thing that
everybody shares. No matter what you're going through, it
makes you forget about your problems. I think the world should
keep laughing."* ~ Kevin Hart

Fourteen years ago, I had the rare opportunity to join a surgical technician program at a large hospital that was offered to individuals with a medical background. Out of two hundred candidates who applied for this advanced training, I was one of the thirty-five were accepted. Perhaps, my ten-year background as a certified medical assistant finally paid off? Whether getting accepted was based on my professional experience or happened to be favor from God, I was thrilled to start this new venture.

Following a month of anatomy, medical terminology, and intense bookwork, our teacher scheduled each student to job shadow with an expert surgical technician. Job shadowing is when someone interested in a particular profession follows around a person who currently has the occupation. On the morning of the job shadow, I headed to the operating room in my blue scrubs. In apprehension, I prayed, *"Dear Lord, please help me to have courage as I move forward in my training. Allow this to be a positive learning experience."*

Feeling nervous and excited to observe surgery for the very first time, I entered the operating room and introduced myself to the charge nurse. In effort to maintain a sterile procedure, I stood by the RN and was in total awe watching all of the professionals in action. After an attendant wheeled in the female geriatric patient, I discovered the woman was being prepped for a hemorrhoidectomy, which is a surgery to remove hemorrhoids.

This is when I knew God had a funny sense of humor. What were the odds that I would end up job shadowing for rectal surgery? In any case, it turned out that hemorrhoid surgery doesn't always mean a stuffy environment. Picture this. Lively conversation, upbeat music flowing from the speakers, and an OR team working side by side, joking as if they were at a family reunion. All the while, the patient's bare bottom was exposed. Good heavens, what a hoot! It took every ounce of self-control for me to not burst out giggling.

Immediately, it had me thinking that God isn't an uptight, grumpy stern man who expects us to live a boring, somber life with complete seriousness. Instead, I think laughter is God's medicine in which He lightens up the mood, especially in awkward situations, such as rectal surgery. We were never meant to be dull, depressed, or despondent. When we observe trials and tribulations in our world, there's even more reason to lighten the heavy load. Sometimes life gets tough and it's disheartening. Never mind happiness; what we genuinely need is joy and laughter!

Multiple scientific studies reveal that laughter produces "feel good" endorphins, which can improve our emotional and physical health. Here are some benefits of laughter:

- Strengthen our immune system
- Boost our energy levels
- Reduce pain
- Relieves stress
- Relaxes our muscles
- Adds joy and zest to life
- Eases anxiety and fear
- Improves our mood

- Lowers blood pressure
- It can help tone our abs
- Produces a general sense of well-being
- Increases a positive attitude
- It can strengthen relationships
- Helps us cope with difficult situations
- Attracts others to us

What I love about joy and laughter is that it's contagious. It overflows into the lives of others. We can't keep it to ourselves. Have you ever noticed that when someone's giggling, you usually join them? Laughter spills over to touch other lives in such a marvelous way. People want to be around us when we are having a good time and enjoying ourselves. We lift their spirits!

Are there areas within your life where you need genuine joy, such as in your home, workplace, or relationships? Today, if laughter and joy is missing consider creative ways to boost your sense of humor. Compile a list of doable steps you can take to bring more laughter and joy into these specific areas. For example, set aside quality time with your friends or family to play board games, go bowling, watch a comedy, or participate in an enjoyable activity. It's time to let your hair down and have some good old fashioned fun!

QUESTIONS TO TRANSFORM:

1. Were you ever in an uncomfortable situation in which laughter helped to break the ice?

2. When was the last time you had fun? What activity were you involved in?

3. List your favorite ways to relax and enjoy yourself.

4. What creative ideas do you have for adding more

laughter and joy into your life?

*"A joyful heart is good medicine, but a crushed spirit dries up
the bones."* Proverbs 17:22 (ESV)

And Sarah said, *"God has made laughter for me; everyone who
hears will laugh over me."* Genesis 21:6 (ESV)

*"Then our mouth was filled with laughter, and our tongue with
shouts of joy; then they said among the nations, "The Lord has
done great things for them." The Lord has done great things for
us; we are glad."* Psalms 126:2-3 (ESV)

*"He will once again fill your mouth with laughter and your lips
with shouts of joy."* Job 8:21 (NLT)

CHAPTER FIFTEEN

You Were Created for a Purpose

*"If you can't figure out your purpose, figure out your passion.
For your passion will lead you right into your purpose." ~*
Bishop T.D. Jakes

From the beginning of time, we were destined for a purpose. Deep within each one of us lies talent, abilities, and strengths that go far beyond our wildest imagination. Too often, we sell ourselves short by thinking, *"I can't do that"* or *"I'm not capable of_____"* (fill in the blank). We fear failure so we simply don't bother to take the risk of trying something new. We hide our true potential behind a mask of self-doubt and trepidation, choosing to "play it safe", instead of appreciating all we are meant to be.

Although we can go a lifetime unaware of our divine purpose, I believe it's crucial to our emotional and spiritual development to walk in this beautiful plan in order to enrich our lives to the fullest. Otherwise, we may find ourselves floundering, questioning why we are here on earth, and feeling as if something is missing. Have you ever wondered why your life hasn't turned out the way you had originally planned? Or felt utterly frustrated about not reaching your true potential within a particular time frame?

In the spring of 2010, I had been prescribed Ativan (Benzodiazepine) to treat insomnia and fibromyalgia. Within a few short months, I experienced intense cognitive impairment along with memory loss. My negative symptoms were so severe that I could no longer focus, think clearly, or recall basic information, such as my phone number. By summertime, I knew something was terribly wrong. This was when my lifelong passion for writing came to a screeching halt.

During atrocious brain fog, my love for writing died. It wasn't that I didn't want to write. Rather, the lack of cognitive function hindered my ability to do so. Based on the fact that writing was such a big part of who I was and my calling in life, when I couldn't follow this dream, a piece of my heart shattered. It was like a dear friend passed away. Darkness and grief consumed me. I missed writing. I missed this creative outlet of expressing myself with pen and paper.

No longer certain of my purpose, I began to lose hope. Sinking low, I questioned what I was good at. Did God have a backup plan for me? How could my cognitive impairment be part of His purpose? Getting through each day was hard work. Barely existing, it took every ounce of strength to manage my physical and emotional pain.

Six months later, after I was discharged from the hospital, God nudged me to get back to writing. Although I lost confidence in myself and didn't believe that I could write something worth publishing, the Lord moved powerfully behind the scenes to prove me wrong. This is when I realized that we can't question God's timing, purpose, or plan for our lives. In our own eyes, we may not fully grasp His omnipotence. We most certainly don't always "get it", despite how much effort we put into over-thinking what He's doing and why He's doing it.

God's purpose can't be derailed by our weakness or troubles. Our frustrating problems will not trip Him up or cause Him delays. Unrelenting hardships, which may bring us to our very knees will not baffle our Creator. His majestic plan is sovereign. In reality, He could use anything to graciously bring us to His place of destiny.

Reinventing You! Simple Steps to Transform Your Body, Mind, & Spirit

One valuable gem I learned through this experience is that living God's purpose is at the very core of our existence. We are not put on earth by accident. We were each created with special talents to be used for a specific purpose. No matter who you are, where you are from, or what your age is, everyone has a unique gift, strength, and calling.

To live a transformed life is to discover what you enjoy the most personally, professionally, and spiritually. It's empowering to live productively with a passionate purpose. By tapping into your hidden strengths and God-given gifts, you'll have a much clearer vision to achieve realistic goals.

How can you be sure of God's calling? How do you know your God-appointed mission in life? We rarely recognize our purpose overnight. Not to say this couldn't happen, but the Lord usually reveals it to us gradually. If you want to know His will, ask for wisdom, pray, listen, and patiently wait. In Romans 12:6-8 (NIV), we are reassured that we're each created with special gifts. *"We have different gifts, according to the grace given to each of us. If your gift is prophesying, then prophesy in accordance with your faith; if it is serving, then serve; if it is teaching, then teach' if it is to encourage, then give encouragement; if it is giving, then give generously; if it is to lead, do it diligently; if it is to show mercy, do it cheerfully."*

Here's a list of other ways to gain more clarity into your life purpose:

- Go to your local community college to take an interest test.
- Read *Strengths Finder 2.0* by Tom Rath at http://strengths.gallup.com/110440/about-strengthsfinder-20.aspx.
- Put into consideration your core values, beliefs, and

priorities.
- Ask your friends, family, and those closest to you what they believe you are naturally good at.
- Consider what you are most passionate about.
- What are your hobbies?
- Who do you most want to help?
- What causes or organizations do you strongly believe in?
- If you had to teach someone, what would you teach?
- Think back to your childhood and recall what you wanted to be when you grew up.
- Who inspires you most?
- Hire a life coach to gain more insight and get unstuck.
- What brings you joy and excitement?
- Listen to your intuition.
- Consider helpful websites geared for self-assessment, such as *The One Question* at http://www.theonequestion.com/
- Read the Bible and pray for discernment.

My favorite book of the Bible is found in Psalms. What I love most about it is that David had a heart for God even when he reached rock bottom. After David fled Saul and hid in a cave, he cried out to His Heavenly Maker asking that his purpose to be fulfilled. Imagine that. You are on the run from evil people who wish you harm and right in the middle of your mess you don't ask for food, water, or safety. Instead, you step out wide to boldly ask God to fulfill his purpose for you. David wept, "*I cry out to God Most High, to God who will fulfill his purpose for me.*" Psalm 57:2 (NLT)

Just as God had a purpose for David in ancient times, He has a divine purpose for you, too. If you've had a dream deep inside of you, don't just ponder the dream you have; decide that you are going to make it happen! Trust that whatever God may have started in you (even if it's been decades), He can bring it to completion. If He's called you to do something (no matter how bizarre, radical, or impossible it may appear on the outside), He will most certainly equip you to fulfill it. *"And I am certain that God, who began the good work within you, will continue his work until it is finally finished on the day when Christ Jesus returns."* Philippians 1:6 (NLT)

What I love most about stepping into God's purpose is that we come alive! There's a deep sense of fulfillment and joy. When we're in alignment with His will, we become energized, excited, and feel at peace about doing what Christ calls us to do. This truly gives our lives meaning and purpose. Having a sense of meaning and purpose not only builds our confidence, but it can help us to find our authentic voice and live true to ourselves. When we are in alignment with our passionate purpose, we become fearless and unstoppable.

If you haven't tapped into your hidden strengths, talents, and God-given gifts, now is the time to explore what you are good at, what you enjoy doing, and whatever you're passionate about. One way of knowing this is by asking others who you trust, by listening to that soft, still voice within you, and by experiencing positive energy when you tap into the areas where you shine best.

If you closely tune into yourself, you may already know what you're good at. Before you can confidently share it with others, you need to unleash your uniqueness. Bravely reinvent yourself. Appreciate your magnificent qualities. Acknowledge them. Value them. Own them. Most importantly, get a crystal clear image of yourself and each of your special gifts. Accept and embrace how Christ designed you by releasing your inner sparkle so you may shine brilliantly!

Reinventing You! Simple Steps to Transform Your Body, Mind, & Spirit

QUESTIONS TO TRANSFORM:

1. As a little girl, what did you want to be when you grew up?

2. What are two of your innate strengths? Do you use them on a frequent basis? If not, what is holding you back from making the most of your natural strengths?

3. Journal your deepest dreams and honestly share what you most hope for.

4. Are there any activities or hobbies that energize and excite you? Could it be transformed into a career?

"Now to Him Who...is able to carry out His purpose and do superabundantly, far over and above all the we dare ask or think, indefinitely beyond our highest prayers, desires, thoughts, hopes, or dreams." Ephesians 3:20 (AMP)

The Lord Almighty has sworn, "Surely, as I have planned, so it will be, and as I have purposed, so it will happen." Isaiah 14:24 (NIV)

"The Lord make his face to shine upon you and be gracious to you;" Numbers 6:25 (ESV)

"Each of you should use whatever gift you have received to serve others, as faithful stewards of God's grace in its various forms." 1 Peter 4:10 (NIV)

DIY FACIAL MASK

It may be surprising that something you probably have in your pantry, such as baking soda, can be an inexpensive way to nourish, protect, and heal the skin on your face. A simple baking soda face mask can clean your skin, kill a wide variety of potentially destructive pathogens, and help you feel a lot better. Baking soda not only promotes smoother, cleaner, and fresher skin, but it can be quite effective. The price point is an excellent alternative to spending a small fortune on high end beauty products. Another perk is that a DIY baking soda facial mask can help clear up stubborn acne and rashes.

Benefits of a DIY Baking Soda Facial Mask:

- The primary benefit is to eliminate blemishes and adult acne because baking soda is a natural antibiotic that can treat the root cause of a potential fungal infection.
- Baking soda can help draw out the infection that causes blackheads and slough off the dry tissue making it easier to extract.
- The baking soda facial mask is great for clogged pores because it has a mild antiseptic and anti-inflammatory properties to ease inflammation, reduce large pores, absorb oil on your skin, and help your skin appear brighter, smoother, and flawless.
- Baking soda makes a top-notch exfoliation to remove the top layer of dead skin cells.

DIY Baking Soda Facial Mask Recipe and Directions:

- Mix 1 tablespoon of cool water with 1-1/2 tablespoons of baking soda.
- Smooth over your face. (Avoid your eye area.)

- Leave on your skin for 5 to 10 minutes. (For sensitive skin, less time is best.)
- Rinse well with warm water.
- With your skin moist from the water, apply your moisturizer.

DIY Baking Soda and Lemon Facial Mask Recipe and Directions:

- 1-1/2 tablespoons of baking soda.
- 1 teaspoon of fresh lemon juice. (Another option is lemon essential oil, which is more concentrated and you only need 5-6 drops.)
- Use whichever ratio works best for you. If you want your mask to be creamier, add more lemon juice. For a thicker consistency, use less lemon juice.
- Mix ingredients together and apply directly to your face. (Avoid eye area)
- Leave on your skin for 5 to 15 minutes. (For sensitive skin, less is best)
- Rinse well with warm water.
- With your skin moist, apply your moisturizer.

CHAPTER SIXTEEN

Listen to Your Body

*"Most of us have become deaf to our own bodies, which is why
we are out of tune."* ~ Terri Guillemets

Yesterday, when I was at the mall shopping for my daughter's birthday, I saw a one of my neighbors from where I used to live. As we chatted, he mentioned that his wife, Ann, had been diagnosed with stage four cancer. He said it caught them by surprise, but they were both hopeful. However, the prognosis for Ann was quite disheartening. Despite chemotherapy, her oncologist said she would only live three to six months.

This devastating news had me wondering how many years Ann may have experienced symptoms related to her cancer, yet she never connected the dots to consider something was seriously wrong? My best guess is that if she's in such a late phase of this fatal disease than logically it means the cancer began years ago. It most certainly didn't happen overnight. Of course, this leads me to wonder if she ever listened to her body.

While I am disheartened that Ann has a short time to live, it has me thinking about how many of us don't listen to our body's internal signals. Are we so wrapped up in our busy lives with far too much on our plates that we ignore internal signs screaming for our attention? Aches and pains are not a "normal" part of life. Constant migraines should not be pushed aside. A lump on our breast should never be ignored with wishful thinking that it will go away on its own.

The truth is that our body is very intelligent. It gives us signals all of the time. They are little warnings alerting us to take action and find a solution. When our stomach growls or we start to feel shaky, it's telling us that we are hungry and should eat. If our body feels bloated or full, it says to stop eating. We need to honor this intrinsic signal and listen to what our body is telling us.

Another red alert that something is wrong is if we get a stuffy nose, sore throat, or puffy eyes. Perhaps, our pizza and ice cream fest that we had over the weekend is an indicator of a potential food allergy or sensitivity? If dairy continues to be a digestive issue, the one helpful way to listen to our body would be an elimination diet. To know for certain if dairy or lactose is the culprit, stop consuming it for at least two solid weeks. (Check your medications, supplements, and various foods or drinks because some may contain traces of dairy.)

Following the elimination diet, reintroduce dairy or lactose into your diet. Keep a food journal to track your physical, emotional, and cognitive symptoms. If the stuffy nose, sore throat, tummy aches, bloating, constipation, migraine, or puffy eyes surface, good chance you can have an allergy or intolerance to dairy. Take heed by tuning into your body and avoiding ingredients that cause you problems.

How many of us are running ourselves ragged and are depleting ourselves because we take on more than we can humanly manage? We do not need to be Wonder Woman and juggle a dozen tasks. When we feel exhausted, why are we relying on large amounts of caffeine or energy drinks to keep going? For heaven's sake, why do we keep doing this to ourselves?

From now on, let's give ourselves permission to rest. If we need to take a nap or go to bed earlier, the kindest act we can do for ourselves is to relax. No guilt. No excuses. No neglecting what our body needs.

If we experience brain fog or clouded thinking,

especially long-term, it's time to ask ourselves what may be the root cause. This doesn't mean covering up our signs or symptoms with harsh chemicals. Rather, it would make more common sense to first take a closer look at our diets, lifestyles, sleep patterns, and stress levels. For example, could the sugar-free soda containing Aspartame be causing negative side effects or directly hindering our health? Are we consuming too much fake foods, sweets, or unhealthy snacks?

I'm not suggesting we become a paranoid hypochondriac with every ache or pain. What I am saying is that our body will tell us what it needs. The key is to pay attention and build awareness. Attention to the human body can bring healing and regeneration. Listen to your gut intuition. If our nation would slow down and become aware of what their bodies are signaling, we would increase our well-being.

Life is short. Take care of your health now. Please do not wait, until you've been diagnosed with _____ (fill in the blank with every imaginable disease or disorder). Stop thinking that at some other time you will get your life together, or begin a healthier eating plan, exercise, lose weight, or change your lifestyle to take better care of yourself.

Today, make the most of every opportunity to improve your body, mind, and spirit by tuning into your internal signals. You don't know when you will take your last breath. Your health is a gift. Your life on earth is precious. There's no better time than this moment to honor the amazing temple God gave you to promote longevity and joy.

QUESTIONS TO TRANSFORM:

1. Did you relate to the true story about Ann who was diagnosed with stage four cancer? Have you, your friend, or loved one experienced a similar situation?

2. When your body sends you signals, how do you respond?

3. What steps can you take to nurture and take better care of yourself?

4. How can you honor your body as a temple of God?

How do you know what your life will be like tomorrow? Your life is like the morning fog—it's here a little while, then it's gone." James 4:14 (NLT)

"Hear, you peoples, all of you, listen, earth and all who live in it, that the Sovereign Lord may bear witness against you, the Lord from his holy temple." Micah 1:2 (NIV)

"Get wisdom, get understanding; do not forget my words or turn away from them. Do not forsake wisdom, and she will protect you; love her, and she will watch over you. The beginning of wisdom is this: Get wisdom. Though it cost all you have, get understanding." Proverbs 4:5-7 (NIV)

"Or do you not know that your body is the temple of the Holy Spirit who is in you, whom you have from God, and you are not your own? For you were bought at a price; therefore glorify God in your body and in your spirit, which are God's." 1 Corinthians 6:19-20 (NKJV)

CHAPTER SEVENTEEN

Our Thoughts Are Powerful

*"Taking care of your thoughts is at least as important as taking
care of your body - if not even more important."*
~ Felix Brocker

Last winter, we experienced freezing temperatures in
Pennsylvania, which included icy conditions. Due to the frigid
weather, my husband, Tony, was temporarily laid off of work.
As a supervisor in construction, he was in the beginning stages
of a new outdoor project. Although we have dealt with similar
situations in the past, it had me worried. On the first day he was
home full-time, my thoughts started racing. I couldn't stop
wondering, *"How are we going to manage our financial
responsibilities without his steady income? How long will this
last?"*

One day of missed work turned into one week, which
soon led to another week of being laid off. I wanted to support
Tony in his stressful situation so I kept my concerns to myself.
Yet deep down inside I was extremely upset over his loss of
income and how this would dramatically impact our family's
future. What started out as a legitimate concern started to unravel
into a never ending thread of worrisome thoughts. Negative
words. Fear. Anxiety. Sleepless nights. Doubting God.

At this point, my thought—life had gone from bad to
worse. Okay, I confess. My thoughts went straight into the
gutter. Based on the fact that I'm not the bread winner in our
family, I was scared about another financial crisis when we were
still shoveling ourselves out of a deep rut from Tony being laid
off two years ago. Being dirt broke is hard. Losing your home to

foreclosure is even harder. My family has been there and done that. It's not an easy circumstance to face, let alone rise above it.

One morning, I awoke with a heavy burden on my shoulders. This is when it occurred to me that my thought—life was destroying my health, sleep, relationships, mind, and faith. No doubt, the enemy knew my weakness. He was quite sly whispering lies to me. Destructive words, spoken and unspoken, were a stronghold on me. He mocked me by saying, *"You're headed for another financial disaster. You will never get ahead. You may as well give up hope because you're going to lose everything!"*

Regardless that Tony wasn't working steady or able to collect unemployment, I needed to put a halt to my stinking thinking, which blew out of control. My imagination went wild and the enemy filled my head with every possible negative scenario, including being homeless. This is when I said enough is enough.

Prayerfully, I sought refuge in my Heavenly Father asking for His protection and provision. With God's Word as my mighty weapon, I rebuked the devil to take back authority over my thoughts. In the Bible, it teaches that we have the ability and authority to take captive every thought. *"We demolish arguments and every pretension that sets itself up against the knowledge of God, and we take captive every thought to make it obedient to Christ."* 2 Corinthians 10:5 (NIV)

Within days of asking God to take my thoughts captive and leaning onto His promises, the weather cleared up and Tony went back to work. It's amazing how one shift in our attitude, thoughts, and perspective can powerfully transform an outcome from being bad to good. The golden nugget of truth is that our thought-life matters to God. What we think, silently or verbally, matters to our overall health; body, mind, and soul.

Reinventing You! Simple Steps to Transform Your Body, Mind, & Spirit

Perhaps, you've been experiencing stressful events in your own life? Maybe you're battling the enemy with stinking thinking? Never underestimate the power of your thoughts. Your words, beliefs, and statements that you say out loud or in silence can either strengthen your soul or leave you empty.

Your thoughts have the power to control; your being, your emotions, your health, your soul, and the way you view the world that surrounds you. Today, be more aware of your thoughlife. Use the Bible to arm yourself. Courageously, take captive every single negative thought that rears its ugly head. Speak scriptures out loud to reaffirm vibrant health, peace of mind, and joy.

QUESTIONS TO TRANSFORM:

1. Recall a circumstance in your own life in which your thoughts spiraled out of control. Write down on paper or share with the group how you handled this situation.

2. Have negative thoughts ever popped into your mind and influenced the way you feel towards someone or something?

3. How can you become more aware of your thoughts and attitude?

4. When your imagination goes wild, what simple steps can you practice to rein in stinking thinking to promote peace of mind?

"Above all else, guard your heart, for everything you do flows from it." Proverbs 4:23 (NIV)

"You were taught, with regard to your former way of life, to put off your old self, which is being corrupted by its deceitful

desires; to be made new in the attitude of your minds." Ephesians 4:22-23 (NIV)

"Finally, brothers and sisters, whatever is true, whatever is noble, whatever is right, whatever is pure, whatever is lovely, whatever is admirable—if anything is excellent or praiseworthy—think about such things." Philippians 4:8 (NIV)

"My thoughts are nothing like your thoughts," says the LORD. *"And my ways are far beyond anything you could imagine."* Isaiah 55:8 (NLT)

CHAPTER EIGHTEEN

Faith Under Attack

"Saints and martyrs are famous for testifying to the truth about Jesus Christ while their enemies set them on fire, but each day ordinary Christians experience small martyrdoms when they blow the whistle on a dangerous product, or lose a friend they had to confront, or stand up in a small group and, for the first time in their lives, say to a group of strangers, "If we suffer persecution and affliction in a right manner, we attain a larger measure of conformity to Christ, by a due improvement of one of these occasions, than we could have done merely by imitating his mercy, in abundance of good works."
~ John Wesley

As a woman of faith, I have been aware of Christianity being under attack in other countries. Through the daily news and media, we hear about violence, beheadings, and every form of evil to those who stand up for their religious beliefs. There are courageous people who will lose their lives as martyrs because of some relation to their faith.

Recently, I had a small taste of my own religion under attack. On Facebook, I had shared a woman's blog about a controversial topic that had gone viral. It pertained to a celebrity who claimed to be a professed Christian, yet had undergone sex reassignment surgery. When I shared my religious views with Bible scriptures pertaining to what God says versus what the world says, I received an onslaught of offensive, hateful comments. Within minutes, I was barraged with vicious criticism and threats that were meant to oppress me from sharing my religious beliefs.

Reinventing You! Simple Steps to Transform Your Body, Mind, & Spirit

We live in an era where groups of people are intent on demoralizing, demeaning, and denouncing Christians as well as what we stand for and believe. Their vigorous tactic is meant to intimidate and shame us by name calling. Their motive is to have us back down from our faith and God's Word. For us to deny that we follow Jesus.

In America, we can openly say we're a Christian, yet the moment we take a firm stance, look out! Once we confidently share our values, beliefs, love for Jesus, or quote Bible verses, naysayers who oppose our faith may ruthlessly belittle, shame, and scorn us. In many cases, whatever we say or do may be used against us and twisted out of proportion.

The persecution we are experiencing is not a surprise. 2 Timothy 3:1-5 (NLT) warns us of the end of times by stating, *"...in the last days there will be very difficult times. For people will love only themselves and their money. They will be boastful and proud, scoffing at God, disobedient to their parents, and ungrateful. They will consider nothing sacred. They will be unloving and unforgiving; they will slander others and have no self-control. They will be cruel and hate what is good. They will betray their friends, be reckless, be puffed up with pride, and love pleasure rather than God. They will act religious, but they will reject the power that could make them godly. Stay away from people like that!"*

Although we don't know when the world will come to an end, we can be certain of this:

- It will come like a thief in the night. The Bible states, *"For you know quite well that the day of the Lord's return will come unexpectedly, like a thief in the night."* 1st Thessalonians 5:2 (NLT)
- There will fierce persecution in which many Christians

will be killed for their faith. *"Then they will deliver you up to tribulation and put you to death, and you will be hated by all nations for my name's sake."* Matthew 24:9 (ESV)

When confronted with this harsh truth, we must ask ourselves five important questions:

1. Is my faith strong enough to keep me rooted when persecution comes?
2. Am I able to trust in God's goodness even during difficult trials?
3. How much suffering and pain is worth saving my soul?
4. Would I be willing to lose my life in effort to save someone else?
5. If I were told to deny my faith or die, what would I choose?

Perhaps, you have experienced hostility and criticism when you openly share your Christian values or beliefs? Dear friend, the Lord has told us to take up His cross and to follow Him. He also said that we will confront trouble, but to take heart because Jesus overcame the world. Today, if you are sensing your faith is under attack, I pray you have dependence on God. May you courageously walk in humble reverence of Him and boldly stand firm in your faith.

QUESTIONS TO TRANSFORM:

1. Do you openly share your faith and religious beliefs? If not, what prevents you from doing so?

2. Have you ever experienced ridicule or harassment for sharing your faith? If so, how did you handle it?

3. If you were told to deny your faith or die, what would you choose?

4. How can you strengthen your faith in effort to keep rooted when persecution comes?

"Stand firm against him, and be strong in your faith. Remember that your Christian brothers and sisters all over the world are going through the same kind of suffering you are." 1 Peter 5:9 (NLT)

"If you try to hang on to your life, you will lose it. But if you give up your life for my sake and for the sake of the Good News, you will save it. And what do you benefit if you gain the whole world but lose your own soul?" Mark 8:35-37 (NLT)

"For all the nations of the world seek after these things, and your Father knows that you need them. Instead, seek his kingdom, and these things will be added to you. Fear not, little flock, for it is your Father's good pleasure to give you the kingdom." Luke 12:30-32 (ESV)

"So never be ashamed to tell others about our Lord." 2 Timothy 1:8 (NLT)

AROMATHERAPY AND ESSENTIAL OILS

Essential oils are the liquids used in aromatherapy. They're made up from the oils of plants, trees, flowers, or other compounds. Although essential oils cannot cure us, these amazing compounds can be valuable healing tools for our physical, emotional, and spiritual health. From biblical days to the present, essential oils have been used for a wide variety of reasons ranging from minor ailments to major diseases. Whether it's allergies, cramps, depression, insomnia, rashes, nausea, colds, or migraines, the list is endless. Truly, there's an essential oil for every concern.

These are my favorite essential oils and how they have benefited my overall wellness:

- **Frankincense essential oil** - Frankincense is my favorite "go to oil" for reducing chronic pain. It's considered *liquid gold*. Also, it's an anti-inflammatory, analgesic, antifungal, and antidepressant. Frankincense essential oil is ideal for treating fibromyalgia, inflammation, insomnia, depression, and neurological disorders. Each morning and night, I rub a few drops of it mixed with fractionated coconut oil directly onto my tender spots. Sometimes if I'm feeling stressed out or need to unwind after a hectic day, I diffuse Frankincense and the rich, woody aroma produces relaxation. When I encounter a fibro flare or back pain, I ingest one to two drops of Frankincense inside a veggie capsule to alleviate inflammation. Please take note that not all brands of essential oils are FDA approved to consume orally. Also, not all essential oils are created equal. Read labels and warnings before ingesting or using essential oils.

- **Patchoulie essential oil** – While it's much loved today, Patchouli essential oil became extremely popular during the 1960's hippie generation. It has powerful qualities for being an antibiotic, antidepressant, anti-inflammatory, fungicide, aphrodisiac, antiseptic, and sedative. Patchoulie is not only an excellent natural alternative for ADD/ADHD, but also for anxiety, Alzheimer's disease, and autism.

- **Vetiver essential oil** – I have experimented with various oils to promote attention, memory, organization, focus, and staying on task. Two excellent essential oils for improving my ADD/ADHD include Vetiver and Patchouli essential oils. Vetiver has a woody aroma, is a thicker oil, and reminds me of tree sap. It's great for reducing anger, anxiety, arthritis, rheumatism, insomnia, and increasing focus. While some people have experienced the sedative qualities of Vetiver for sleep, I have personally not had similar results. Instead, I believe this oil has helps me to remain alert, focused, and it greatly increases my ability to be productive while I work.

- **Lavender essential oil** – Lavender is known for its pleasant aroma and is naturally antiseptic and antiviral, which can be used for bites, cuts, stings, bruises, rashes, or skin irritations. For insomnia, I've had phenomenal results using Lavender essential oil as it's very soothing and relaxing. Usually, I diffuse a few drops of Lavender essential oil in the evening to promote tranquility and I rub a drop or two on the bottoms of my bare feet. Due to Lavenders calming properties, it has been used for alleviating insomnia, anxiety, depression, restlessness, and stress. You can put a few drops in a diffuser in your bedroom, add to your bath water, or apply topically to your skin before going to sleep to create a relaxing environment.

- **Clary Sage essential oil** – Clary Sage essential oil is extracted by steam distillation from the buds and leaves of the Clary Sage plant whose scientific name is Salvia Sclarea. The health benefits of Clary Sage can be attributed to its properties as an anticonvulsive, antispasmodic, antiseptic, aphrodisiac, astringent, bactericidal, digestive, and sedative. Due to my severe nature of sleep issues with fibromyalgia, I pulled out the big guns, which led to discover calmative properties of Clary Sage. While this oil may be geared toward females to address PMS, menstrual cramps, and menopause, it's also quite effective as a sleep aid, antidepressant, and balancing moods. (Caution: Never use Clary Sage essential oil when drinking alcohol.)
- **Oregano essential oil** – Oregano essential oil is a popular alternative treatment for colds, flu, and viruses, which is best achieved by adding a few drops to a diffuser and inhaling. Another option is to add a few drops of oregano oil into a veggie capsule and mix with a carrier oil to dilute it, as this oil is considered "hot". The health benefits of Oregano essential oil can be attributed to its properties as an antiviral, antibacterial, antifungal, anti-parasitic, antioxidant, anti-inflammatory, digestive, and an anti-allergenic substance. Some people use it for respiratory conditions, digestive issues, or candida infections. (Caution: Do not apply Oregano essential oil directly to your skin without a carrier oil to dilute it.)
- **Ginger essential oil** – Aromatically, Ginger essential oil is spicy and warming. Although it's well suited for fall and winter months, I use it year round. Topically, Ginger oil can be useful in blends and formulas intended to improve circulation. It's a frequent addition to blends for massage, arthritis, and muscular aches and pains. The

warming and soothing qualities of Ginger essential oil help address digestive issues, such as a tummy ache, morning sickness, motion sickness, vertigo, nausea, heartburn, diarrhea, gas, and spasms. Emotionally, I find Ginger oil energizing and uplifting. During sickness, when you can't take fluids by mouth, you can rub a few drops of Ginger essential oil directly onto your stomach or tired muscles. Otherwise, you can ingest a few drops of Ginger oil inside a veggie capsule. For those with sensitivities, you may consider mixing it with a carrier oil before using orally.

- **Peppermint essential oil** – Peppermint essential oil has an uplifting aroma in which it's suitable for an abundance of oral and topical uses. It works wonders for the body and mind. Peppermint essential oil is so powerful that a mere whiff can help you become energetic and mentally alert. It can provide a cool sensation and has a calming effect on the body, which can relieve sore muscles when used topically. In addition, it has antimicrobial properties so it can help freshen bad breath, soothe digestive distress, reduce nausea, and is a great natural remedy for morning sickness as well as motion sickness. Fortunately, Peppermint essential oil can also help to clear congestion, soothe headaches, and ease symptoms from PMS.

The best location to apply essential oils are on the soles of your feet because they absorb quickly into your bloodstream. Other topical areas are your wrists, inner arms, behind your knees, along your spine, and at the nape of your neck. Pure essential oils are very concentrate so a small amount goes along way. For best results of pure essential oils, use on a consistent basis.

IMPORTANT: Most essential oils are safe and free of adverse side effects when used properly. However, as with any substance you are introducing into your body, it is important to use them intelligently. Keep in mind that not all brands of essential oils are equal. In addition, not all brands of essential oils can be used internally. If you have sensitivities, always use a carrier oil to dilute the essential oils before using topically or orally. If you are nursing, pregnant, take prescriptions, or you have a medical condition, please consider seeking medical advice before using essential oils.

Also, do your own research to gain more insight into the benefits and cautions for specific essential oils. While there are many warnings about the safe use of essential oils, they are amazing natural remedies when used correctly. You may consider finding a trained aromatherapist, herbalist, or naturopathic doctor to inquire about specific questions about essential oils. Lastly, it's very important to use essential oils that are pure and of a superior quality.

CHAPTER NINETEEN

Hold the Gluten!

"We each know our bodies better than anyone else does – any doctor, any prescription, any diagnosis. It takes time, patience, and a positive attitude to keep your head up and stay strong until you find all the answers to your body's wants and needs. For some it can be a long, long road to find that balance – but there is always a shiny, bright light at the end of the tunnel."
~ Amie Valpone

This was me in my 40s: Fatigued, frumpy, forgetful, and despising the reflection I saw in my mirror. Silently, I struggled with hormonal imbalances, G.I. distress, memory loss, nonstop bladder infections, kidney stones, severe chronic pain, and every imaginable craving. It was not until I discovered my gluten intolerance that I realized my diet needed changed. Of course, for me it wasn't an overnight success; it was more like a yearlong battle.

My common sense told me to make healthy dietary changes and eliminate gluten. At the same time, my old habits were hard to break. Mid-afternoon meltdowns led to devouring chips, chocolate, and junk food to soothe my frayed nerves. As a devoted Starbucks lover, I relied on fancy coffee to get me through slumps when I was tired or couldn't focus.

During Christmas 2011, I caved in by consuming delectable cookies, pies, and goodies. Feeling guilty and ashamed with my lack of self-control, I justified that it was the holidays and sweets were part of the celebration. By January 2012, I became very ill from gluten and unhealthy ingredients. This led to six horrible weeks of being home bound with disabling symptoms.

It was much more than tummy troubles. Rather, my nasty symptoms were muscular aches and pains from a fibromyalgia flare up, severe constipation, bloating, brain fog, insomnia, depression, lack of concentration, extreme fatigue, headaches, acne, and over twenty inflamed ulcers inside my mouth. They were the lesser of two evils. The most excruciating symptoms involved burning sensations similar to a urinary tract infection, except it was not a UTI. Repeated medical tests revealed negatives results for bladder and kidney infections.

Additional symptoms included urinary urgency, frequency, pelvic pain, low lumbar pain, and abdominal pain. The urge to urinate was so intense that I ran to the toilet every five minutes. This led to sleep deprivation and anxiety, which only compounded my physical and emotional torment. Numerous visits to the emergency room and urologist resulted in a diagnosis of Interstitial Cystitis (IC), which I truly believe was severe gluten intolerance mimicking IC. When the gluten ingredients were eliminated, my negative IC symptoms gradually disappeared.

As you can imagine, my poor health took a toll on my body, mind, and spirit. In desperation, I cried out to Jesus for help. During sleepless nights, I prayed for him to give me real solutions to lead me onto a new healing path. What I discovered is God wants His children to not only pray and seek His wisdom, but to step out because faith without action is dead. (Read James 14-26 ESV)

Through research and educating myself about celiac disease (CD), gluten intolerance, and a clean diet, I started taking necessary action steps to improve my overall quality of life. Out of each possible area to make positive health changes, I believe *nutrition* is the first place to start. The foods and beverages we consume on a daily basis will either help or hinder our overall health. If we want to be well, we must closely examine our lifestyles, especially nutrition.

Although I wanted to be tested for celiac disease, my family didn't have medical insurance at that time. Without health coverage, my next best choice was to simply change my diet and eat gluten-free. In essence, it's the same solution for those who receive a positive test result for CD.

Your immune system, which God designed to attack things like viruses and bacteria, thinks that those molecules are invading organisms, which attacks them and surrounding tissues. Celiac disease is a genetically linked autoimmune disorder that can affect children and adults. It's a condition that damages the lining of the small intestine and prevents it from absorbing part of food, which is important to stay healthy. The damage is due to consuming gluten, which is found in wheat, barley, spelt, rye, and oats.

Gluten consists of two proteins; gliadin and glutenin. The gliadin part is what people negatively react to. The gluten protein is not normally found in the human body so that is where the trouble begins. Typically, it gets into our body when we ingest gluten, but there are other methods, such as licking the glue on the envelope to seal it.

When you think of gluten, imagine *"glue"* and its sticky consistency. Without gluten, homemade bread wouldn't be thick and chewy. Gluten is not only contained in foods and drinks, but also in personal care products, natural supplements, medicine, beer, condiments, chewing gum, toothpaste, dental floss, and the list is endless. You don't have to look far because gluten is lurking on most of the shelves in our grocery stores.

Following a restricted gluten-free (GF) diet is no easy task. Gluten is in almost everything and it takes much work to protect oneself. It's quite challenging when dining out because restaurants don't always adhere to a strict protocol in the kitchen. Even though a wide range of restaurants claim to have a GF menu, when you look closely at the fine print, most restaurants will not guarantee the safety of their foods and beverages. They use a disclaimer to legally protect themselves. It's great for them, but unfortunate for those who must maintain a restricted GF diet. Dine out at your own risk!

From my experience, cross-contamination happens in the kitchen when staff uses the same deep fryer for regular foods and/or uses pots, pans, utensils, and the same prep area which come into contact with gluten. This may lead to sickness ranging from mild to extremely severe reactions for those who have celiac disease and/or a gluten intolerance. You can never be too careful.

Once I gained insight into CD and gluten sensitivities, I cleaned up my diet. It required a major overhaul. I reinvented myself. It took me nearly two years to adjust to a new way of life. On many occasions, I accidentally consumed gluten resulting in a severe illness. Truth be told, I ventured into a GF lifestyle kicking and screaming.

Here's the undeniable fact: Reinventing yourself isn't always easy. Sometimes it's the most difficult process, especially when it comes to eating your favorite foods. I missed juicy hamburgers, thick pizza, delicious pancakes, and having the freedom to eat whatever I desired. Realistically, I was forced to not only clean up my diet, but I needed to change my oral, beauty, and personal care products to prevent coming into contact with gluten ingredients. Fortunately, I found awesome GF toothpaste, floss, lipstick, mascara, hand lotion, and body wash that I love.

In addition to eating GF, I prefer organic and whole foods. Following my new way of life, I made major changes impacting where I shop and what I purchase. In order to live a cleaner, organic lifestyle, I eliminated undesirable ingredients. The list of dangerous ingredients is extensive and it includes genetically modified organisms (GMO), pesticides, steroids, antibiotics, preservatives, monosodium glutamate (MSG), artificial colors and flavors, artificial sweeteners, chemical additives, and processed food.

The bottom line is that I'm striving for vibrant health. In the process, I've become more conscious of how I'm living and what I am consuming. The goal is to help myself not only be well, but to remain physically and emotionally healthy to avoid illness.

If you're wondering why your parents or grandparents didn't have these same kinds of ailments from foods, I think the main reason is because they ate traditional home cooked meals from scratch. If we take a closer look at what they consumed on a daily basis, it wasn't like it is today. They didn't have processed, genetically modified organisms with added stabilizers, chemicals, food coloring, artificial flavors, preservatives, antibiotics, artificial sweeteners, or steroids in their foods. Simply stated, our food industry is nothing like it used to be. Today, this can explain why our nation has become very sick

Perhaps, you or a loved one are struggling with digestive concerns, brain fog, mood swings, muscular pain, inflammation, unexplained rashes, an auto-immune disease, or fatigue? Along with seeking clarity and wisdom, you have four options:

1. Do nothing and make no changes in which you may never know if you have a gluten intolerance or celiac disease.
2. Schedule an appointment with a gastrointestinal specialist for medical testing.
3. Start an elimination diet in which you remove wheat, rye, barley, spelt, and oats to determine if your health may improve or your symptoms may subside within 30 to 90 days.

4. Educate yourself about celiac disease and gluten intolerance. Discover as much information and facts as you can from credible resources, including alternative medicine, naturopathic physicians, holistic nutritionists, or a wellness coach specializing in CD and clean nutrition.

QUESTIONS TO TRANSFORM:

1. Do you have food sensitivities or allergies? If so, how has this influenced the way you eat?

2. Are you a bread or carb lover? If so, have you experienced any negative symptoms that may be from consuming gluten?

3. Has anyone in your family or yourself been diagnosed with celiac disease or a food intolerance? If so, was it initially difficult to make the transition to eliminate these foods?

4. If you suspect that you may have a sensitivity or problem with ingredients, are you ready to take the next step to gain more awareness and clean up your diet?

"Gluten-free is more than the latest fad...there are multiple studies showing that gluten can cause harmful effects, especially long-term." ~ AuthorityNutrition.com

"Remember the old "this is your brain" anti-drug campaign with the egg sizzling in a fry pan? Think of this as the celiac/gluten-sensitive equivalent: "This is your brain – and this is your brain on gluten." ~ AllergicLiving.com

"After I was diagnosed with Celiac Disease, I said yes to food,

*with great enthusiasm . . . I vowed to taste everything I could eat,
rather than focusing on what I could not. "* ~ Shauna James Ahern

CHAPTER TWENTY

Intimacy With God

"It's not about an organized religious system, it's about a supernatural, intimate relationship with the creator God of Christianity." ~ R. Alan Woods

What many people do not know about me is that I spent most of my life not knowing God rather than being in an intimate relationship with Him. From early on, I wasn't raised in church or any form of religion. When I was two years old my parent's divorced. Following their breakup my single mother sought comfort through her Catholic church. Unfortunately, the priest rejected her. Instead of reaching out to my mom with compassion, he spoke harsh words of condemnation. On that dismal day, she vowed to never step foot into a church again.

For over twenty-nine years, I lived a secular lifestyle and was caught up in the world. While I had moments in which I yearned to know God more, I felt that most religions enforced strict rules. Each time I tried to read the Bible, I couldn't understand scriptures. Seriously, it seemed as if I were reading Chinese. Despite my efforts, the Bible was foreign to me.

On the rare moments when I did attend church, I found it utterly dull and far too stuffy. Most of these traditional churches were built on a set of firm rules and regulations. They didn't teach the love of our heavenly Father. Instead, they portrayed a dictatorial God with legalistic religion based on a clear set of man-made rules. Those who disobeyed were scorned and cast out from the church.

Perplexed by this rigid religion, I wanted no part of it. As far as I was concerned, I didn't fit in, nor did I want to conform to their stifled practice. The truth is that not all churches are friendly. At least not the ones that I visited. The people were not compassionate, welcoming, or accepting of outsiders. Nobody spoke about salvation. Ever. There was no redemption message. Not one single sermon. No forgiveness of sins. Grace didn't exist.

Instead, the congregation sat quietly in the pews with no expression on their faces, hands tightly folded, and the fear of God in them. You know that look...like a deer in the headlights. How come those churches were filled with obligation and fear, rather than love, grace, and mercy? In a place where Jesus Christ should be experienced for the hopeless, lonely, and lost, how come I never sensed Him in my presence?

Feeling disillusioned, I resisted all forms of religion. It was easier to keep God at an arms-length away from me. While I prayed and believed in Him, I didn't truly know Him in an intimate way. Looking back on my day of redemption in 1992, I'm most grateful to my sister who shared Christ with me. After six months of repeated invitations to visit her church, it was a moment of desperation that led me there.

In complete awe. I was thrilled with this quaint church. This church was different from the churches in my past—they were warm, welcoming, and non-judgmental. When the pastor spoke, my eyes filled with tears as I heard for the first time that Jesus died on the cross to give me everlasting life. To save me; a messed up gal with a rocky marriage who was lonely and broken. In one simple prayer, my sins were forgiven and I was made new.

What I learned through the years is that God desires us to know Him intimately; the Father, Son, and Holy Spirit. It's not about a brick and mortar building; it's about one faithful God. We are not meant to get caught up in legalism, rules, or religion. Rather, the Lord wants us to simply bask in His presence, to know *Him* more.

Reinventing You! Simple Steps to Transform
Your Body, Mind, & Spirit

Knowing Jesus and drawing close to Him can happen in our everyday lives. You don't need to be in a certain place, with a certain group of people, or pray at a special time each week, to know God. Having an intimate relationship with Christ looks more like this. Waking up each morning and greeting your heavenly Maker as if He were right next to you. Talking to Him as you brush your teeth. Giving thanks to Him when you sip your tea. Praising the Lord as you drive to work listening to your favorite band. Chatting with Him while you fold your laundry and have an ongoing dialogue between the two of you; one on one. Intimacy with God happens in the ordinary moments when we quiet our souls to soak into His presence.

It's a conversation that happens throughout your day and night. Although, it doesn't have to be intentional or constant, I believe the more you know God, the more frequently you find yourself sharing your heart, your pain, and your concerns with Him. Having an intimate relationship is no longer about following a set of religious obligations or adamant rules.

Whether you're a church-goer or not, Jesus wants a relationship with you. Do not allow your lack of participation in a formal setting prevent you from seeking Christ. While I do believe church can enhance our knowledge, understanding of Him, and biblical teachings, you can still have an intimate relationship with the Lord whether you are a regular church goer or not.

Jesus died and rose three days later so we could have a thriving relationship with Him; not a set of narrow rules that we're forced to follow. God designed us for a supernatural intimate relationship. This requires open communication. He wants to talk with us, walk with us, and help us to grow in our faith.

The intensity of His love for us is beyond our comprehension. It's unlike any other love on earth. The deeper we go to know Him more, the closer we are to Him to experience His glory. Our Abba Father is wooing us from heaven, whispering, *"Come to me and draw close, my dear daughter."* James 4:8 (NKJV)

God does not ask that you change yourself before you commit to Him. He wants you to come just as you are. To recognize your need to have your sins forgiven. To accept His free gift of forgiveness that He has offered to you through His death on the cross. Right where you are sitting this very moment you can call out to Christ and ask for Him to come into your life. Trust that He's pursuing you and yearns to hear your voice. On bended knees, say, *"I want to know You more, Lord."*

Keep in mind, just as developing a close relationship with another person takes time, so is intimacy with God. As you grow in your faith and believe His promises, your love for Him can become increasingly rewarding, precious, and abundant.

QUESTIONS TO TRANSFORM:

1. Were you raised in a particular religion or church? If so, how did this influence your childhood? If not, did you desire to go to church?

2. Does reading the Bible ever seem like it's a foreign language or hard to understand? Which version do you prefer?

3. In what tangible ways can you deepen your intimacy with God?

4. Have you accepted Jesus' free gift of salvation? If not, are you ready to do so?

"Draw near to God and He will draw near to you." James 4:8 (NKJV)

Reinventing You! Simple Steps to Transform Your Body, Mind, & Spirit

"Then you shall call, and the Lord will answer; You shall cry, and He will say, 'Here I am.' Isaiah 58:9 (NKJV)

"The Lord is near to all who call on him, to all who call on him in truth." Psalm 145:18 (ESV)

"Now this is eternal life: that they know you, the only true God, and Jesus Christ, whom you have sent." John 17:3 (NIV)

CHAPTER TWENTY-ONE

Transformation Requires Self-care

*"Self-care is never a selfish act - it is simply good stewardship
of the only gift I have, the gift I was put on earth to offer
others. Anytime we can listen to true self and give the care it
requires, we do it not only for ourselves, but for the many
others whose lives we touch."* ~ Parker J. Palmer

Looking back on my own recovery process and transformation to regain my health, it required daily self-care. According to Dictionary.com, self-care is *"Care of the self without medical or other professional consultation."* From my experience, self-care is actively engaging in the activities that may help us to gain or maintain optimal wellness; to enhance our body, emotions, and spiritual health. In simpler terms, it's doing what we can do with what we have on a consistent basis to improve our entire being. This proactive approach can place us in a better position to heal and eventually to thrive.

Over the course of seven years, when I consider how I got from there to here, it wasn't one particular method helping me along the healing path. Rather, it was multiple therapeutic, self-care strategies, which proved highly beneficial. My overall condition improved from being disabled and homebound to becoming healthier and independent.

This doesn't mean that I'm cured of fibromyalgia, depression, or damage done from harsh chemicals. It means that despite my challenges, I've gained better insight to lead a higher quality of life. More so, I actively sought practical life-style changes to improve my physical, emotional, and spiritual well-being. Each one was like finding a missing piece of a puzzle, which gradually led to restoration.

In a nutshell, self-care is an empowering expression of *self-love*. Despite our failings and weaknesses, we learn to love ourselves and view ourselves as worthy. We care about our well-being. We love ourselves in such a positive way that we flourish. Do you know what it looks like to love yourself?

During my darkest and gloomiest moments, self-love was not easy. It wasn't automatic. Having a hissy fit came easier for me. I've learned the hard way that how I responded to stress greatly influenced my health; for better or for worse. Caring for oneself and loving oneself requires diligence. It can evolve through time.

Here's what I've discovered about self-care and self-love:

- Loving ourselves means taking good care of our body, mind, and spirit.
- Caring for ourselves is not selfish.
- Self-care and self-love require being true to ourselves.
- By being true to oneself, we create healthy boundaries.
- We let go of people pleasing.
- Listen to our body's signals to eat, sleep, reduce stress, pray, be still, etc.
- Follow our gut intuition.
- No rehashing past mistakes, experiences, or regrets that can hinder our progress.
- Take responsibility for our own thoughts, behaviors, habits, and actions.
- Pray for wisdom, discernment, and ask God for guidance.
- Refuse to seek permission or approval to be ourselves.
- Give our body the nurturing, rest, exercise, and comfort it needs to the best of our ability.

- Be honest with ourselves about our strengths and weaknesses.
- Take time to grow spiritually and connect to God on a deeper level.
- Allow ourselves to feel what we feel without berating ourselves or feeling guilty.
- Strive for self-improvement, yet accept ourselves right where we are now.

Consciously, we choose to give ourselves the gift of self-care. To honor, respect, and love the precious life in which God gave us, including the good, the bad, and the downright painful. It's an enriching process of self-growth that can lead to acceptance. We may not like how we look or feel right now, but we can come to terms with it. We may despise our aches and pains, emotional meltdowns, or cellulite, yet we go beyond the superficial to love and care for ourselves fully.

Regardless of our age or season in life, at some point we may find ourselves carrying heavy burdens. Extra stress. Broken relationships. Losses. Disappointments. Isolation. Illness. Grief. The list is endless. Any way we look at it, carrying heavy burdens, especially over a lengthy period of time, can take a toll on us. To move forward to healing, it will entail self-care.

Before I explain practical steps to achieve self-care, let's first cover the basics of what self-care isn't. Self-care is not:

- Getting intoxicated with alcohol
- Indulging in street drugs
- Abusing pharmaceutical medications
- Self-harm or injury
- Binging and purging
- Destructive behaviors or lifestyles
- Neglecting our safety and/or health

Self-care is a set of practices that help you feel nourished physically, emotionally, and spiritually. Self-care is taking time to refresh, renew, and recharge in a manner that is meaningful to you. Based on the fact that we each have our own likes and dislikes as well as unique personalities, self-care may differ from person to person. For example, an introvert may desire to be alone and still for self-care whereas an extrovert may want to be in a social environment and active during self-care.

As for myself, I've always been a social butterfly as an extrovert. However, during my initial recovery process when I was tapering harsh chemicals and going through wicked withdrawals, I preferred solitude. I sensed that in order to be true to myself and honor the dark place where I was at (Ativan withdrawals), I would respect my difficult season.

In my early stages of healing, this is what my self-care involved:

- **Journaling** - In search of peace, I journaled. It was freeing to release all of my hurt, frustrations, and baggage. Journaling gave me the opportunity to vent, cry, and analyze the bumpy road I traveled. Expressing my inner thoughts and feelings were a godsend. With pen and paper in hand, I ranted about my harrowing trials. It felt good to let go of negative energy. I poured out my heart on paper. I wrote my deepest dreams and aspirations. Most importantly, journaling provided positive benefits by reducing stress, clarifying thoughts, effectively solving problems, exploring my strengths, praying for God's will, and increasing my awareness of hidden blessings. Journaling became a blissful sanctuary. A safe place to be real. No pressure or worry about being harshly judged. It brought calm to my storm. New insight. Peace of mind. Personal growth. This amazing form of self-care powerfully awakened my inner voice.

- **Gratitude** – In effort to improve my outlook on life, I started compiling a list of things that I was grateful for. Cultivating an attitude of gratitude begins with counting our blessings. Gratitude is expressing thanks for special blessings we receive. When life gets hectic and we feel overwhelmed, we can take a moment to focus on the people or situations we are most grateful for. When we have an attitude of gratitude other things will fall by the wayside. The more we are grateful for what we have, the more we can live fully in the present. When we live in the present moment, the greater we build stepping stones for a brighter future. Being thankful helps us to take into account all of the positive in our lives. It gives us a whole new perspective.

- **Soothing Sounds** - During long nights when I was plagued with insomnia, I dimmed the lights and listened to music, which promoted relaxation. One CD combined flowing, ethereal music with soothing sounds of waves lapping against the shore. Closing my eyes, I was magically transported to a tropical island where I could envision sea gulls flying overhead, feel the warm sun radiating on my skin, and picture myself walking barefoot on the beach. A cool breeze ruffled through my hair as I knelt down to pick up a beautiful sea shell. As I listened to its tranquil sound of ocean waves, blissful peace gently washed over me. Other musical options included soothing soundtracks of calming atmospheres, strings, piano, and guitar. For stress relief, some people enjoy nature music with the soft pitter-patter of raindrops, birds singing in the distance, or flowing waterfalls. While your preference may vary, choose a style of soothing sounds that resonates within your own spirit.

- **Tranquility and Aromatherapy** – Sometimes when I felt sad, anxious, or restless, I created a relaxing environment by lighting candles or diffusing pure essential oils to encourage solitude. My favorite scents for aromatherapy were Lavender essential oil (relaxing and stress reliever), Bergamot essential oil (calming and uplifting), and Wild Orange (joy and peace). If my fibromyalgia was flaring and I hurt all over, I would soak in a hot bathtub filled with Epsom salts and a few drops of Lavender essential oil. It was very common for me to light scented candles around the tub to simply relish in the tranquil atmosphere. In my experience, this form of self-care made a world of difference; physically and mentally.

- **Praise and Worship Music** - There were many occasions in my recovery when I listened to contemporary Christian music. By taking time to worship and praise God, I removed the focus off of my problems. Instead of worrying about negative situations where I had no control, I gave my utmost attention to Jesus. During worship and praise, I avoided distractions. It was a serene moment to escape TV, text messaging, and surfing the Internet. It was simply me and God. Quiet time when I lost myself as the Holy Spirit wrapped me in His tender arms. Singing my heart out, my troubles and frustrations melted in His presence.

- **Home Spa** – A sure way to lift my spirits and help me to feel better about myself is personal self-care; otherwise known as girly girl pampering. It's amazing how a little bit of lip gloss, flat ironing my hair, and a pedicure dramatically transformed me from feeling blah to exuberant! I'm a huge believer that when we physically look better, we emotionally feel better. Taking time for personal hygiene and adding a little pampering into my

self-care routine most definitely boosted my attitude and
self-confidence.

- **Positive Affirmations** – At first, this felt a bit awkward
  for me, but I started saying positive affirmations out loud
  or writing them down on index cards as little reminders
  that I was healing. An affirmation is a statement or
  phrase that we declare is true. The purpose of verbally
  saying daily affirmations is to motivate, encourage, and
  inspire our own selves. Regardless of the present
  situation, we state what we desire the outcome to be. It's
  kind of like faith...being sure of what we hope for and
  certain of what we do not see. (Hebrews 11:1) I would
  wake up in the morning and say, *"God blesses me with a
  sound mind."* Or I would affirm, *"Today, I am one step
  closer to healing."* For those who battle pessimism or
  negative self-talk, the kindest act of self-care you can
  provide for yourself is positive affirmations. While it can
  take effort and consistency, ultimately it could increase
  your self-esteem and self-worth.

- **Clean Nutrition** – Along my wellness journey, it
  became very clear that I needed to clean up my diet to
  improve my moods, memory, and physical health. I
  learned about specific foods and drinks that could help
  me to decrease my inflammation, digestive issues, and
  pain. Through a series of time, I gained wisdom,
  knowledge, and insight into the truth about genetically
  modified organisms (GMO), artificial sweeteners,
  processed foods, gluten, and how it overall affected how
  I functioned on a day to day basis. For me, self-care
  meant loving myself enough to bravely say, "No", to the
  ingredients that were hindering my progress. It opened
  up the doorway to saying, "Yes", to whole, pure, organic
  nutrition, which greatly increased my quality of life.

Reinventing You! Simple Steps to Transform
Your Body, Mind, & Spirit

I'm not sure how to tactfully write this, but I hope that you will receive it with openness and love. We can't go through life neglecting self-care by beating up our bodies with nicotine, alcohol, drugs, toxic behaviors/ relationships/lifestyles, destructive addictions, and chronic stress without reaping long-term, negative results. Along the journey in life, our choices do have a significant impact on our future as well as our families.

The good news is you can start over, get a second chance, and actively increase the quality of your health; physically, emotionally, and spiritually. When you take good care of yourself, you are in a better position to take better care of others. While there are only a certain number of hours in each day and you may have many responsibilities, it's important that you carve out special time to focus on your self-care. In case you have forgotten or need a gentle reminder: Your life is worth it. *You* are worth it!

The main purpose of self-care is to nurture yourself. To build awareness of your physical, emotional, and spiritual needs. To advocate for vibrant health. Self-care is not merely existing on earth or barely surviving. Rather, self-care is *intentionally* taking the best care of yourself in order to transform your health to fully thrive.

QUESTIONS TO TRANSFORM:

1. What prevents you from focusing on self-care? Do you believe it's selfish to care for oneself?

2. In which tangible ways do you provide self-love?

3. Do you find yourself caring for everyone else's needs? Is nurturing yourself difficult? If so, journal or share with the group how this impacts your physical, emotional, and spiritual health.

4. How can you realistically improve your self-care on a consistent basis? Exactly what action steps will you need to take in order to make this happen?

"Rest and self-care are so important. When you take time to replenish your spirit, it allows you to serve others from the overflow. You cannot serve from an empty vessel." ~ Eleanor Brownn

"Much of your strength as a woman can come from the resolve to replenish and fill your own well and essence first, before taking care of others." ~ Miranda J. Barret

"Come to me, all you who are weary and burdened, and I will give you rest. Take my yoke upon you and learn from me, for I am gentle and humble in heart, and you will find rest for your souls. For my yoke is easy and my burden is light." Matthew 11:28-30 (NIV)

"I will refresh the weary and satisfy the faint." Jeremiah 31:25 (NIV)

ORGANIC COCONUT HAIR TREATMENT

Organic, virgin coconut oil is rapidly growing in popularity for a wide variety of uses and benefits. For everything from shaving your legs to moisturizing your skin to removing mascara, this miracle oil is the cream of the crop for enhancing beauty naturally. The oil of the coconut is comprised mainly of smaller medium-chain fatty acids. It's the only oil that will penetrate the hair shaft, rather than simply coat it. The benefit is that coconut oil will moisturize, repair, and condition your hair from the inside out. In addition, coconut oil is far more superior compared to other oils and conditioners.

You can use organic, virgin coconut oil as a leave-in treatment to repair split ends, add a healthy shine to dry hair, or moisturize your scalp. The longer you leave coconut oil on your hair the more effective it will be. Yes, you can even sleep with it on your hair, but be sure to wear a shower cap to keep your pillow clean.

As far as which brand of coconut oil to choose, everyone may have their own preference. As for myself, I have experimented with a wide variety of reputable brands. My daughter and I both love Trader Joe's brand the best. It's not only a high quality, but the price point is affordable.

Coconut Oil Treatment Directions:
- Use a small pan with water at the lowest heat on your stove. (Only fill up 1/2 way.)
- Place the entire glass jar of coconut oil into the warm water of the pan.
- Once the coconut melts, carefully remove from the pan.
- Pour 1 cup of the melted coconut oil into a bowl. (Avoid plastic.)

Reinventing You! Simple Steps to Transform Your Body, Mind, & Spirit

- To stimulate hair growth, add 1-2 drops of Rosemary Essential Oil to the bowl of coconut oil.
- Once your coconut oil comes to room temperature and is still melted, use your fingers to gently massage the oil onto your dry hair, especially focusing on the ends if they are damaged or brittle.
- Work through with a comb or hair pick. (You want it well distributed, but not dripping.)
- Wrap your hair with a soft towel or a shower cup to keep the oil off of your clothes.
- Leave it on for at least 30-60 minutes, but a few hours is best.
- One option is to leave it on overnight.
- Wash the coconut oil out of your hair, shampoo, and use a regular conditioner.

CHAPTER TWENTY-TWO

Is Your Food Helping or Harming You?

"Today, more than 95% of all chronic disease is caused by food choice, toxic food ingredients, nutritional deficiencies and lack of physical exercise." ~ Mike Adams

Are you overwhelmed, frustrated, and tired of conflicting advice on nutrition, healthy ingredients, or dieting? Do you read labels, but feel as if you are reading a foreign language because you don't understand what the words mean? Have you wondered if your food and beverages are connected to your health or weight concerns?

If you were to start a food diary to compile everything you consume on a daily basis, what would stand out the most to you? Would your list reveal that you have a sweet tooth? Love fried foods? Enjoy hearty homemade cooking? Adore gourmet coffee? Or the local pizza shop knows you by name?

In my experience, I discovered that what I consume really does matter, especially if it's a consistent pattern. Four years ago, I came to the conclusion that something had to change or else I would never regain my health. I had to ask myself this: Was my wellness important enough for me to change my eating habits? Could I increase my overall quality of life (physically and emotionally) if I eliminated specific ingredients from my diet?

Had I not suffered or lost my health, I don't know if I would have considered making such drastic dietary changes. Sickness can be a motivator for reinventing yourself and changing your diet! In retrospect, I'm thankful for my past illness because it forced me to take a closer look at nutrition and how it could significantly improve my health. In order for me to go from being disabled and afflicted to becoming independent and restored, it required these steps:

- To look outside the box.
- Educate myself about the long-term implications involved in consuming harsh ingredients.
- Do thorough research on a large variety of topics, including clean nutrition, plant-based foods, gluten, GMO, processed foods, etc.
- Build my awareness on natural, gentle options.
- Become my own wellness advocate.
- Determine that my health is my top priority.
- Lean on God for restoration.
- Take the first step of action to make necessary dietary changes.

If I learned only one thing from my impaired condition, it's this: I am responsible for my own health. No one knows my body like I do. How can I expect to stay well and be at my best if I delegate my health to someone else? I challenge you to consider how you can enhance your own body and mind with pure nutrition. Only you can determine the necessary action steps that may lead you to improved wellness. The choice is yours. It's up to each individual to decide for themselves how much their health is worth. I believe that we can't put a price tag on wellness. There's no amount of money that can replace vibrant health.

For those who are interested in making positive changes in their diet, here are ingredients to consider eliminating. Try to have an open mind. If this is new to you, first check it out to gain more knowledge. Please do your own research. Learn as much

as you can about how each one may impact your health for better
or for worse.

10 Ingredients to Avoid:

1. Soda
2. Genetically Modified Organisms (GMO)
3. Artificial Sweeteners
4. Monosodium Glutamate (MSG)
5. Artificial Flavors and Colors
6. Hydrogenated Vegetable Oil
7. High Fructose Corn Syrup
8. Preservatives
9. Sodium Nitrate
10. Processed Foods

Our nation is in a health crisis directly linked to poor
nutrition and overeating. According to the *Centers for Disease
Control and Prevention (CDC),* more than 78.6 million of U.S.
adults are obese. We put toxic fake foods into our bodies, but
wonder why we are sick and depressed. We continue a vicious
cycle of consuming the wrong ingredients along with having a
stressful lifestyle, yet question why cancer is rampant. Most of
our society live in fear and believe they have no control.

My positive message is that we do have control. We need
to take back ownership of our bodies and minds. Do not blindly
eat something without first checking the ingredients to see if
there are potential side effects or long-term damage. Be
conscious of what you're consuming before you go to the
grocery store or dine out.

Most importantly, take the initiative to gain more
knowledge because it will empower you. Understand your options
so you may be in a better position to make an informed choice.
Ultimately, your choices in nutrition can greatly impact your life to

help you *thrive* as a whole person; body, mind, and spirit.

QUESTIONS TO TRANSFORM:

1. Have you ever considered if your foods or beverages are helping or harming you?

2. Do you check ingredients on labels before you go shopping? If not, are you concerned with what you eat or drink?

3. What do pure nutrients mean to you?

4. Have you ever experienced negative reactions to any of the ingredients listed above?

5. Which food or beverage would you avoid if you knew your health could be restored?

"So, whether you eat or drink, or whatever you do, do all to the glory of God." 1 Corinthians 10:31 (ESV)

And God said, *"Behold, I have given you every plant yielding seed that is on the face of all the earth, and every tree with seed in its fruit. You shall have them for food."* Genesis 1:29 (ESV)

"Dear friend, I pray that you may enjoy good health and that all may go well with you, even as your soul is getting along well." 3 John 1:2 (NIV)

"Let food be thy medicine and medicine be thy food" ~ Hippocrates

"The doctor of the future will no longer treat the human frame with drugs, but rather will cure and prevent disease with nutrition." ~ Thomas Edison

CHAPTER TWENTY-THREE

Be Bold and Brave

*"Being brave is about your next step and staying in the present
instead of trapped in the fear of the future or the regrets and
mistakes of the past."* ~ Diane Cunningham

On a cold winter day in December 2013, I took the craziest, bravest step of my entire life. In one click of a button, I released my true story to our world through Kindle Direct Publishing. It was my memoir that shared my darkest battles and rock bottom moments. While a part of me felt confident to share my voice to give others hope, another part of me cringed on the inside with fear. Good Lord, what have I done? What will people say about me? Will they harshly judge me?

While I have never felt so vulnerable and scared, this was by far the most empowering experience I ever had. When I gave myself permission to be bold and brave by launching my first book, it provided me the freedom to just be me. An imperfect woman of faith with wacky ADD challenges who dared to face her fears and have the courage to help others not feel so alone in the middle of their own messy, beautiful lives.

Looking back, my defining turning point happened when I decided to step out of the boat (my ordinary, comfortable life) to write my memoir and say, "yes" to God. In all honesty, it wasn't that I believed in myself or writing skills. Rather, I believed Christ who revealed He wanted me to share my personal journey of rising above adversity. I trusted He would equip me to do it if this was His purpose for my life.

There is something magical and transformational about saying "yes" to God. When you take His hand, step out of that boat (your ordinary, comfortable life), and be brave. Instead of spending your lifetime living in fear and playing it safe, you boldly walk in obedience. God makes you brave. He wants you to trust Him. He calls you out beyond the safety of the boat into murky waters and crashing waves. Fearfully, you hold your breath and dive right in! Waiting on the other side is Jesus with outstretched arms ready to catch you.

The funny thing about being brave is that many women don't give themselves credit where they deserve it. You know who they are—mothers, daughters, sisters, wives, and grandmothers. They are you and me, ordinary females who have special hopes and dreams. The brave women include the single moms working day and night to make ends meet for their children, the courageous woman enduring months of chemotherapy and radiation to treat her cancer, the tear-stained wife who buried her husband after an unexpected death, a brokenhearted bride who was left standing alone at the alter on her wedding day, and the scarred daughter who suffered a freak accident that turned her life upside down, yet each woman boldly rose above opposition.

You see, being brave doesn't mean we will never be scared or uncomfortable. Instead, being brave means we can courageously take on daunting challenges, despite our fears. Oftentimes, we over-analyze situations and our imagination goes wild. We may think of the worst that could happen or misjudge our own ability to overcome hardships. In reality, it's usually not as intimidating as we think once we jump in and do what we fear most.

Being brave means giving ourselves permission to be exactly who we are, rather than having to shape and mold ourselves into someone who we think people want us to be. It means getting in touch with our real, authentic selves and expressing that to the world. It's having the courage to be vulnerable, yet assertive. When we're assertive, it's not arrogant, passive, or hostile. Instead, being assertive is standing up for ourselves with confidence where our "yes" means "yes" and our "no" means "no."

Being Bold and Brave is:

- Allowing yourself to feel what you feel without stuffing your emotions.
- Refusing to play it safe.
- Listening to your gut intuition.
- Trusting that God made you for so much more.
- Being fearless to take the path less traveled.
- Making bold decisions.
- Voicing your opinion on what matters most to you even if others don't agree.
- Asking for help despite your ego begging you not to.
- Facing an uncomfortable issue that you have tried to avoid.
- Saying yes, to God to trust His will for you.
- Standing up for your beliefs, values, and faith.
- When you stop trying to control everything around you.
- Giggling at yourself and the silly mishaps you get into.
- Saying "no" to something you don't want even if it may upset those around you.
- Forgiving yourself for past mistakes.
- Setting healthy boundaries in your life.
- Refusing to allow failures and weaknesses to dictate your future.
- Having the courage to leave toxic, abusive relationships.
- Acknowledging your fears and no longer being ashamed of them.
- Following your passionate pursuits.
- Taking simple steps to reinvent yourself.

Reinventing You! Simple Steps to Transform Your Body, Mind, & Spirit

Today, do one act of courage to show your trust in the One who has you in the palm of His hands. Actively step out of your comfort zone to do what scares you most. Yes, it's risky, but it is also an exhilarating adrenaline rush to empower you to transform your life! What God-size dream is tucked inside your heart? Be bold. Be brave. Take a gigantic leap of faith into the extraordinary!

QUESTIONS TO TRANSFORM:

1. In which areas of your life do you feel the most fearful and vulnerable?

2. Do you worry about what others think of you or what they say about you?

3. List three ways that you could be brave.

4. What God-size dream is tucked inside of your heart? Are you willing to leave your comfort zone to bravely follow this dream?

"Have I not commanded you? Be strong and courageous. Do not be afraid; do not be discouraged, for the Lord your God will be with you wherever you go." Joshua 1:9 (NIV)

"When I am afraid, I put my trust in you." Psalm 56:3 (ESV)

"Arise! For this matter is your responsibility, but we will be with you; be courageous and act." Ezra 10:4 (NASB)

"When I called out to you, you answered me. You made me strong and brave." Psalm 138:3 (NIRV)

CHAPTER TWENTY-FOUR

Small Steps Add Up!

*"The secret of getting ahead is getting started. The secret of
getting started is breaking your complex overwhelming tasks
into small manageable tasks, and starting on the first one."*
~ Mark Twain

As I reflect on the past seven years, I believe my small, daily steps that I practiced added up to positive changes. In the beginning of my wellness journey, I may not have had all of the answers. I didn't know exactly where each step would lead me, but I trusted that moving forward, no matter how slowly, would be better than staying permanently stuck. My physical and emotional healing didn't happen by mere accident. Rather, I took deliberate steps to get me where I am today.

Although I still have fibromyalgia, herniated discs, and food sensitivities, when I take a look back on how I had once lived in chronic, debilitated pain with severe anxiety, depression, insomnia, and brain fog, I am in awe at how far I've come. The woman I was seven years ago is not the same woman today. Similar to a butterfly, I've gone through a metamorphosis, been released from my dark cocoon, embraced my wings, and soared! Who would have imagined that simple steps in my diet, thinking, physical activity, and faith would promote an amazing transformation?

While I ponder this miraculous blessing upon my life, I trust that God was a big part of it. I am eternally grateful and give Him all of the glory. However, I do believe He ultimately called me to step out in my own faith to take action. If I desired real change to occur, it required me to boldly take some risks, be open to new ideas, do research, and to place one foot in front of the other.

Yes, I admit that it was scary and intimidating, but living in torment 24/7 in a body that wasn't functioning properly was far more frightening. Sometimes we have to reach rock bottom before we're willing to rise up and overcome our trials. In my case, I had a choice. Life or death. Heaven or hell. Once I hit bottom in a pit of despair, I knew the only way to go was up. Being hopeless and quitting was not an option. Squeezing my eyes shut, I dived into the deep end of the water where God threw me His anchor of hope.

Of course, this doesn't mean it was easy because there were times when I felt as if I were drowning. On many occasions I floundered and questioned if I was going in the right direction. Each step I took was a trial and error. What it taught me was that my health was worth saving. My mind was worth saving. I was worth saving. Beyond a shadow of doubt, I knew that I was precious to God. My body, mind, and soul mattered to Him. This is what kept me going when I was sinking into murky darkness. To know that Jesus was fighting on behalf of my life to give me a fresh start. He gave me the courage to not give up.

So here I've climbed a steep mountain and overcome unfathomable hardships. I am living proof that the Lord does heal. He gives second and third chances. He renews stagnant faith. He provides a sound mind. God can redeem a broken gal who was close to death and restore her life. As I write this last chapter, I have to stop and grab some tissue. These are happy tears, grateful tears, and healing tears of joy!

You see, my physical, emotional, and spiritual health has dramatically changed for the better. When something this awesome happens, you can't keep it to yourself. Instead, you want to reach out and share it with those who need it most. You want to make a positive difference in the lives of others. To offer people simple steps to healing, health, and hope.

Reinventing You! Simple Steps to Transform Your Body, Mind, & Spirit

Last year, God pressed my heart to write this book, and as a topic that I believe in passionately, I answered His call. Yet, I realized that change isn't easy, especially for women who are busy taking care of their families, working full-time, carrying heavy burdens, and burning the candle on both ends. As I sought clarity and wisdom, it became clear that females from all walks of life are desperate for help, but unsure of where to begin.

For this reason, I've come alongside women to encourage, equip, educate, and empower them to take small steps to transform their lives. There's a saying that it takes twenty-one days to form a habit. While this could be true for some people, I believe that it doesn't apply to everyone. I can guarantee you, it took me more than twenty-one days to form my own healthy habits. The truth is that we each have our own personalities, responsibilities, medical histories, and circumstances. We are unique. Therefore, the length of time in forming new habits may vary from person to person.

Based on my experience, I believe small steps add up and can make a big difference. For example, when I decided to get physically fit, I discovered that going gung ho by working out for one hour caused me severe pain. My body was screaming, *"Stop!"* For an entire week, I suffered the consequences and couldn't exercise. It taught me that one hour is not ideal for me. Rather than overextend myself, it made common sense to create small fitness goals, such as doing gentle stretching in the morning and walking on my treadmill for thirty minutes in the afternoon. I was more likely to stick with this goal if my body wasn't hurting all over.

When we take a closer look at our lives physically, emotionally, and spiritually, we may get overwhelmed and uncertain of what changes to consider. The thought of switching things up can cause our heart to race. By nature, we usually avoid change and want to stick with our regular routines.

However, in order to improve each area within our lives, we may need to consider realistic modifications.

We live in a society that has a microwave mindset. We want everything fast. Yesterday wasn't soon enough! We want a quick fix without having to work at it. We yearn for instant gratification, but if something takes too long, we quit or move on to something else. Instant gratification is making us perpetually impatient. The demands for quick results is seeping into every corner of our lives.

The secret of making lasting change is to acknowledge and accept that *real* change takes time and patience. We didn't get chronically ill overnight. We didn't gain weight in one week or even one month. Good chance, it may take us longer than twenty-one days to overcome whatever we're facing. Whether it's something physical, emotional, spiritual, or a combination, we may need to be realistic in our goals for meaningful change to happen. The first step is getting started!

Tips to Taking Small Steps:
- Consider making one or two small changes per month.
- For overachievers, aim for one small change weekly.
- Break big goals into baby steps.
- Implement your little steps gradually.
- Track your progress on paper with dates and accomplishments.
- Give yourself a reward for your progress at least once a month.
- Take one day at a time and try not to rush the process.
- If you fall off the wagon, give yourself grace, brush yourself off, and start fresh the next day.
- Make yourself accountable for your actions, thoughts, and behaviors.

Reinventing You! Simple Steps to Transform Your Body, Mind, & Spirit

- Have specific goals and keep it simple.
- Be brave by asking for help when needed.
- Post your written goal where you can see it daily.
- Focus on progress, not perfection.
- Create your goals so they are measurable.
- Be realistic in your expectations and time line of completing your goals.
- Keep it simple by focusing on one tiny step at a time.
- Celebrate small victories!

While you desire lasting change with positive results, it will take commitment from you to transform your dreams into a reality. Be aware that there can be tough moments when you're ready to throw in the towel. Frustrating times when you may want to quit. When it gets rough or you hit a roadblock, you must forge ahead and keep going. Despite blood, sweat, and tears, do not give up on yourself. You are worth the fight for a brighter future!

Bestselling novelist, Sarah Dessen, sums it up nicely by saying, *"It shouldn't be easy to be amazing. Then everything would be. It's the things you fight for and struggle with before earning that have the greatest worth. When somethings difficult to come by, you'll do that much more to make sure it's even harder—or impossible—to lose."*

Obtaining wellness naturally is truly a lifestyle in which you take the best care of yourself. It's when you become the CEO of your body, mind, and spirit. Although your approach to wellness may not look identical to mine, we share a common goal. We want to flourish and feel good about ourselves. I pray that you courageously choose to make your overall health a priority and gain more confidence in yourself. May you take simple steps to have vibrant health, a sound mind, deeper faith, and live a life filled with enthusiasm, purpose, and peace as you reach your full potential.

Reinventing You! Simple Steps to Transform Your Body, Mind, & Spirit

QUESTIONS TO TRANSFORM:

1. Why is the first step always the hardest? How do you motivate yourself to take the first step?

2. Can you break your steps into manageable tasks?

3. By nature, do you like making changes or avoid it like the plague?

4. What is one change that you want to work on this month?

5. Do you reward yourself for small victories? If not, how come? If so, how do you reward yourself?

"The LORD directs the steps of the godly. He delights in every detail of their lives." Psalm 37:23 (NLT)

"A person plans his course, but the Lord directs his steps." Proverbs 16:9 (NET)

The Lord says, "I will guide you along the best pathway for your life. I will advise you and watch over you." Psalm 32:8 (NLT)

PROFESSIONAL RESOURCES

Author/Speaker/Coach

Beth Jones – She is an International Speaker, Amazon Best Seller Author, wife to paramedic Ray Jones, and mom of three beautiful daughters. Her inspiring signature talk is about the fairy tale of Cinderella and her glass slippers, relating it to your big dreams coming true and fulfilling your unique purpose. Beth's mission is equipping women to use their gifts for God, doing what they love, and prospering in all areas of life. You can follow her on Periscope and Twitter at @bethmjones or connect with her on her website at: http://www.bethjones.net

Dana Arcuri – A captivating author, speaker, and wellness coach who delivers a powerful message on healing, health, and hope. She equips, educates, and empowers women to take back control of their lives to fully thrive. Dana is passionate about empowering others to transform their own physical, emotional, and spiritual health through wellness coaching. For encouragement and wellness tips, please visit her website and Facebook author page: http://danaarcuri.com

https://www.facebook.com/DanaArcuri

Benzodiazepine and Cymbalta

Benzodiazepine Support Group – An online forum to connect with others experiencing similar challenges with benzodiazepines.

http://www.benzobuddies.org/

Joan Gadsby – Is recognized internationally as an authority, consultant, lecturer, and speaker on the responsible and informed use of benzodiazepines and anti-depressants. She is the author of *Addiction by Prescription: One Woman's Triumph and Fight for Change,* published in 2000. She is also a co-executive producer and research consultant of the television documentary, <u>*Our Pill Epidemic: The Shocking Story of a Society Hooked on Drugs*</u>, available on video and for international broadcast.

http://www.addictionbyprescription.com/

Mad in America – A website designed to serve as a resource and community for those interested in rethinking psychiatric care in the United States and abroad. The purpose is to provide readers with news, recovery stories, access to source documents, and informed writings of bloggers.

http://www.madinamerica.com/

Professor C Heather Ashton, DM, FRCP, Emeritus Professor of Clinical Psychopharmacology – Dr. Ashton operated a benzodiazepine withdrawal clinic for 12 years, is the UK's leading expert on benzodiazepines, and she's the author of *Benzodiazepines: How They Work and How to Withdraw.* The Ashton Manual, including its 2011 update provides a wealth of information pertaining to benzodiazepines, symptoms, tapers, withdrawals, and recovery.

http://www.benzo.org.uk/manual/index.htm

http://www.benzo.org.uk/ashsupp11.htm

Recovery and Renewal – A self-help website with valuable resources pertaining to tranquilizers, benzodiazepines, antidepressants, coping tools, and recovery. The Founder of

Recovery Road, Bliss Johns, is the author of *BENZO – WISE, A Recovery Company,* published in 2009. For those who need to know how to successfully cope with benzodiazepine withdrawal, I highly recommend this excellent book and website, which is filled with valuable information, plus helpful resources.

http://recovery-road.org/

The Tranquillizer Recovery and Awareness Place -
Benzodiazepine Withdrawal Guide.
http://www.non-benzodiazepines.org.uk/withdrawal-guide.html

Drug Secrets: What the FDA isn't telling – Insightful article about the dangers of Cymbalta (Duloxetine).

http://www.slate.com/articles/health_and_science/medical_exa miner/2005/09/drug_secrets.html

Celiac Disease and Gluten Sensitivity

American Celiac Disease Alliance – A non-profit organization that represents and advocates on behalf of the entire celiac community, including patients, physicians, researchers, food manufacturers, and other service providers.

http://americanceliac.org/celiac-disease/

Celiac Disease Foundation – A non-profit, public benefit corporation established in 1990 by Elaine Monarch to support the celiac disease community by funding important advocacy, education, and research initiatives.

https://celiac.org/

Celiac Support Association – A membership association pursuing a mission of helping to optimize the health of those with celiac disease and gluten sensitivities through research, education, and support.

http://www.csaceliacs.org/

National Foundation for Celiac Awareness – Promotes widespread understanding of celiac disease as a serious genetic autoimmune condition and works to secure early diagnosis and effective management. They empower their community to live life to the fullest and serve as a leading and trusted resource that inspires hope, accelerates innovation, and forges pathways to a cure.

http://www.celiaccentral.org/

Gluten Intolerance Group – A non-profit association funded by private donations, membership proceeds and industry programs. It relies on tax-deductible contributions to support its many innovative industry, service, social and awareness programs. They are a highly respected leader in the gluten-free community since it was founded in 1974. In addition to their local branches across the United States, the Gluten Intolerance Group has increased its presence internationally to 27 countries. It is headquartered in Auburn, WA.

https://www.gluten.org/

Gluten Free Drugs – Uncertain if your prescriptions or over the counter medication is gluten-free? Here is a helpful resource in effort to avoid contamination with gluten ingredients. This website is authored and maintained by a clinical pharmacist as a public service, receiving no compensation whatsoever for providing this information. Information for this website is obtained from a number of sources, including personal contact with the manufacturers and input from other individuals who contact manufacturers. The information is continually updated as it is obtained and is for informational purposes only.

http://glutenfreedrugs.com/

http://www.glutenfreedrugs.com/newlist.htm

Eating Disorders

Laurie Glass – Has a Christian counseling degree, a history of anorexia, and a passion to help those with eating disorders. She is the creator of Freedom from Eating Disorders where she offers a Christ-centered recovery course, unique recovery note cards, practical e-books, a free monthly newsletter, and much more. For more information, please visit her website at: http://freedomfromed.com/Thin Within – In 1975, Thin Within workshops were started by Judy Wardell-Halliday and Joy Imboden Overstreet. They both shared past struggles with food and weight-related issues, and from these experiences and their research, they developed a revolutionary approach that has helped thousands with similar problems throughout the United States and Canada. In 1980, Joy left Thin Within to pursue her education in health and nutrition, while Judy continued to run the organization and teach seminars. Thin Within grew to include 10 offices in the western metropolitan areas. In 1994, Judy and her husband, Arthur Halliday, MD, wrote Silent Hunger, which expanded the proven weight management program and included the most essential element of God's grace needed for a permanent solution to disordered eating. Silent Hunger (since republished as Thin Again) emphasizes how the Holy Spirit empowers the individual with God's transforming love and grace to live as a naturally thin person.

http://www.thinwithin.org/

Emotional Health

Dr. Michelle Bengtson - Author, speaker and board certified clinical neuropsychologist, Dr. Michelle Bengtson is also a wife, mother and friend. As a neuropsychologist, she evaluates and treats patients with any kind of neurocognitive disorder ranging from autism to depression to dementia. She knows pain and despair firsthand and combines her professional expertise and personal experience with her faith to address issues surrounding medical and mental disorders, both for those who suffer and for those who care for them. She offers sound practical tools, affirms worth, and encourages faith. Dr. Michelle Bengtson offers hope as a key to unlock joy and relief—even in the middle of the storm. She blogs regularly on her own site:

http://drmichellebengtson.com/

Karen Lindwall-Bourg - An inspired writer, speaker, Biblical Counselor, coach, and consultant and State of Texas approved LPC supervisor leading families, couples, and individuals who are overwhelmed or grieved by life's demands toward inspired and insightful solutions based on the Word of God (*rhemas*) that glorify and honor the Lord along life's journey. She is the founder of RHEMA Counseling Associates in North Texas. All RHEMA counselors and coaches strive to equip families and individuals with tools they can use for years to come, and use practical approaches including guided assignments between counseling sessions to enhance and accelerate the process, which assures lasting results, while keeping it cost effective.

http://rhemacounseling.com/

Peter R. Breggin, M.D. - Psychiatrist and speaker who advocates to reform the mental health field. He is the author of many mental health books, including *Psychiatric Drug Withdrawal: A Guide for Prescribers, Therapists, Patients and their Families*, published in 2013 and *Medication Madness: The Role of Psychiatric Drugs in Cases of Violence, Suicide and Murder,* published in 2008.

http://www.breggin.com/

Fibromyalgia

Aqua 4 Balance - A unique website about aquatic therapy, exercise, and water-based wellness. Their mission is to provide quality content to promote vibrant living for the body, mind, and spirit.

http://www.aqua4balance.com/index.html

Jacob Teitelbaum, M.D. - A board certified internist and nationally known expert in the fields of chronic fatigue syndrome, fibromyalgia, sleep, and pain. Best-selling author of *From Fatigued to Fantastic,* published in October 2007 and *The Fatigue and Fibromyalgia Solution*, published in August 2013.

http://www.endfatigue.com/

Rest Ministries, Inc – A non-profit Christian organization that exists to serve people who live with chronic illness or pain, and their families, by providing spiritual, emotional, relational, and practical support through multiple programs and resources.

http://www.restministries.com/

Fitness

Leslie Sansone's Walk at Home – Over 25 years ago, what started as a few aerobics classes in Leslie's health club has grown into the #1 in-home walking program worldwide with over 18 million DVDs sold. From the very first "Walk Aerobics" VHS tape to their latest best-selling DVDs and downloads, they have produced over 100 in-home workouts.

http://www.walkathome.com/

Grief Recovery

Debbra Bronstad – After finding healing for her own losses, Debbra Bronstad is passionate about helping women experience greater peace, hope, and freedom in the midst of the trials and transitions of life as a Christian Life Coach and Grief Recovery Coach. Unresolved grief, beginning with childhood losses and including later losses can open the door to a host of other life problems, including anxiety, depression, drug and alcohol abuse, and conflicts in relationships. Contact Debbra for a free phone consultation regarding coaching services at 248-929-5354 and visit her link for a free report on the Myths of Grief as well as upcoming free webinars. Debbra resides in Michigan where she also maintains a private practice as a licensed Marriage and Family Therapist.

http://www.stages-of-grief-recovery.com/free-report.html

Journaling

Journaling 4 Faith – Kathy Bornarth, MA, LPC, is a certified Journal to the Self Instructor at Journal 4 Faith and has been journaling for over 25 years. Journaling to grow in faith allows you to examine and record your thoughts. Yet journaling for faith goes a step further. You process those thoughts not only to gain clarity, but also to grow in a deeper relationship with God and experience His healing. This website offers journaling prompts, tips, workshops, and journal coaching.

http://journaling4faith.com/

Naturopathic Physicians

American Association of Naturopathic Physicians – Founded in 1985, the American Association of Naturopathic Physicians (AANP) is the national professional society representing licensed naturopathic physicians. AANP aims to increase awareness of and expand access to naturopathic physicians, help its members build successful medical practices, and expand the body of naturopathic medicine research.

http://www.naturopathic.org/

American Naturopathic Medical Association – The American Naturopathic Medical Association (ANMA) is the oldest and largest American Association of Naturopathic Physicians. Founded in 1981, ANMA is a nonprofit, scientific, educational, organization, dedicated to exploring new frontiers of mind, body, medicine and health.

http://www.anma.org/

The Canadian Association of Naturopathic Doctors – Since 1955, The Canadian Association of Naturopathic Doctors (CAND) has been the national voice of the Canadian naturopathic profession. The vision of the CAND is to be a strong voice in Canadian health care and to ensure the optimal health of Canadians through the active promotion of the art and science of

naturopathic medicine and the advancement of its practice.
https://www.cand.ca/

Non-Toxic Beauty

Campaign for Safe Cosmetics – Since 2004, the Campaign for Safe Cosmetics has uses smarts and sass to pressure cosmetics industry to make safer products. The Campaign for Safe Cosmetics coalition works to protect health of consumers, workers, and the environment through public education and engagement, corporate accountability and sustainability campaigns and legislative advocacy designed to eliminate dangerous chemicals linked to adverse health impacts from cosmetics and person care products.

http://www.safecosmetics.org/

EWG's Skin Deep Cosmetics Database – It's their mission at Environmental Working Group (EWG) to use the power of information to protect human health and the environment. EWG's Skin Deep database gives practical solutions to protect yourself and your family from everyday exposures to chemicals. In2004, they launched Skin Deep to create online safety profiles for cosmetics and personal care products. Their aim is to fill in where industry and government leave off. Companies are allowed to use almost any ingredient they wish. The U.S. Government doesn't review the safety of products before they're sold. The staff scientists from EWG compare the ingredients on personal care labels and websites to information in nearly 60 toxicity and regulatory databases. Currently, in their eighth year, EWG's Skin Deep database provides you with easy-to-navigate safety ratings for a wide range of products and ingredients on the market.

http://www.ewg.org/skindeep/

Gluten Free Makeup Gal – The founder of this website discovered that wheat-based components are very common in makeup, but are not always easy to spot in the lengthy lists of unpronounceable ingredients on the back of cosmetic boxes. She learned that, like food, navigating gluten free through the makeup world is a tricky business, full of ruts, potholes, and dead ends. Her goal is to prevent gluten related illness and discomfort from sneaking in through our makeup. She is passionate about sharing her research, reviews, and discoveries about gluten free makeup.

http://www.glutenfreemakeupgal.com/

Plant Based Nutrition

Plant Based on a Budget – There are a lot of reasons to eat more plants and a lot of misconceptions about what that means. What Plant Based on a Budget offers is affordable, easy, and delicious eating a plant based diet can be, how to shop at specialty grocery stores or restock your pantry with all kinds of unfamiliar products and substitutes, but most importantly, how you don't have to sacrifice time, taste, or money in the pursuit of healthier, tastier eating.

http://plantbasedonabudget.com/

PlantPure Nation – Behind the feature documentary, PlantPure Nation, is a team of dedicated and passionate people working to spread the film and its message to as many cities across the world. PlantPure Nation has also launched a grassroots community-based strategy that engages millions of people everywhere to bring the message of plant-based nutrition to family, friends, and neighbors. Their goal is a world of healthy people, strong economies, sustainable food systems, and an environment on the mend. To find PlantPure Nation in your local community, please visit their website.

http://plantpurenation.com/

Prayer and Spiritual Growth

Just Joy! Ministries – They help women navigate through the journey of life and believe that joy is God's will for every day...for every minute that you are breathing the atmosphere of earth. They are passionate about living with joy through the Word of God, the power of prayer, the intimacy of worship, and the delight of friends. The founder, Carol McLeod, is an author and popular speaker at women's conferences and retreats where she teaches the Word of God with great joy and enthusiasm. Carol encourages and empowers women with passionate and practical biblical messages mixed with her own special brand of hope and humor.

justjoyministries.com

Prayer and Spiritual Care – The Office of Prayer and Spiritual Care serves people seeking help through prayer with a 24/7/365 automated call line, which allows callers to listen to prayers relating to a variety of needs and concerns. Listeners may also hear daily scripture and prayer devotional as well as learn about resources offered by the OPSC. You may contact them at 1-800-477-2937.

http://prayer.ag.org/

The Council – This organization is dedicated to building the largest Christian Prayer Network in the world. The pray engine is for those who have reached a crossroad in their life, need prayer, and direction in which way to go. Your prayer concerns are important to them. Each prayer request they receive is prayed for by a trained prayer warrior by name and by need. All prayer is confidential, free, and available 24 hours a day, seven days a week.

http://www.the-council.org/

The Treasured Woman Network – Karen Jantzi, CPC/CMEC, is the founding president of The Treasured Woman Network and CEO of her own consulting and coaching company. She has a passion for helping women find a permanent sense of self-worth and value through living in the love and authority of Jesus Christ in their lives. She has been a successful business owner and executive for over20 years and enjoys helping women bring life to their dreams of owning a business. As an author, blogger, and speaker, Karen shares her life-changing story of overcoming rejection and abandonment, finding peace in the midst of illness, and beginning again after divorce with women across the nation with the hope that they, too, will turn to Christ and live a life they treasure. You may contact her at 407-687-5988 or karendjantzi@gmail.com.

http://www.treasuredwoman.com/

Suicide Prevention

American Foundation for Suicide Prevention

http://www.afsp.org/

1-800-273-8255

Canadian Association for Suicide Prevention (CASP)

http://www.suicideprevention.ca/

International World-Wide Suicide and Crisis Hotlines

http://www.suicidehotlines.com/international.html

National Suicide Hotlines USA

http://www.suicidehotlines.com/

1-800-784-2433, 1-800-273-8255

Deaf Hotline: 1-800-799-4TTY (4889)

ACKNOWLEDGMENTS

To my Heavenly Father: There are no words that could fully express how much You mean tome and how eternally grateful I am for Your grace. Thank You for being my lifeline to cling to, for Your restoration, and for always being faithful. Without Your guidance, wisdom, strength, and provision, this book would not have been possible.

To my husband, Tony: I sincerely appreciate your love, encouragement, and support during my lengthy writing process. Thank you for your patience and for taking on much more household responsibilities while I was busy writing. Congratulations on taking simple steps to transform your own health by kicking your nicotine habit! Happy one year being smoke-free!

To my children, Anthony, Jenna, and Ryanna: Each one of you are a blessing from God and have given me so much joy. I love you dearly and my life would not be complete without you being a part of it. Through the past few years, it's been amazing watching each of you take necessary steps to increase your own quality of life by practicing natural options, including pure nutrition. High fives to all three of you for building awareness and advocating for your own health!

To my mother, Dolly: You have been my biggest cheerleader in life. From the time I was a young girl, you encouraged me to follow my passion for writing. I'm very blessed with your unconditional love, support, and motivation. Thank you so much for cheering me onward and being my biggest fan!

**Reinventing You! Simple Steps to Transform
Your Body, Mind, & Spirit**

To Christine Dupre: Thank you for expertly designing amazing covers for all three of my books. Also, thank you for creating fabulous images for my author page on Facebook. Your beautiful designs demonstrate exactly what I've envisioned. It has been wonderful working with such a talented expert!

To Michele Jones: When I was preparing for my book launch there were unexpected delays in which I needed to hire a new editor. You were a godsend and the answer to my prayers. Mere words cannot express how grateful I am that I was connected to you. I appreciate your expertise, suggestions, and talent. What a blessing it has been to work with you!

ABOUT THE AUTHOR

Dana Arcuri is a captivating author, speaker, and wellness coach who delivers a powerful message on healing, health, and hope. She equips, educates, and empowers women to take back control of their lives to thrive. Her 50-Day Devotional, *Harvest of Hope*, published in November 2014, encourages women to draw closer to God as they move forward in faith to apply what they learn. Her memoir, *Harvest of Hope: Living Victoriously Through Adversity,* was published in December 2013. In addition, she's a contributing author for *Inspired Women Succeed*, published in May 2011.

As a freelance writer, her work has been published in *Christian Women Lifestyle xPress Online Magazine, Pearls of Promise Ministries, Write Where It Hurts, Seriously Write, Totally Her, American Collegiate Poets, Fall Concours 1984,* and her inspiring quote from her devotional was published on Oprah Winfrey and Deepak Chopra's 21-day *Manifesting Grace Through Gratitude.* Dana has been a featured speaker on several Christian radio shows, including *Moving Forward in Faith* and *Your Journey To Freedom.* In 2015, she had the honor of being nominated as one of 100 Top Faith Blogs for Christian Women on *Women's Bible Cafe.*

Dana has over 25 years' experience working as a licensed beauty expert. Her professional credits include PBS for *Doo Wop 50',* Cornerstone Television for *His Place* and *Getting Together* as well as *Pittsburgh Wedding Pages* and *Gateway Publications.* She leads *Writing Purposely Group Coaching* for aspiring writers and *Be Transformed in 90 Days* life coaching. When Dana's not busy writing, she enjoys snuggling up to a great book, dark chocolate, and building her wellness business.

Connect with Dana

Website: http://www.danaarcuri.com/

Facebook: https://www.facebook.com/DanaArcuri

YouTube: https://www.youtube.com/user/FaithInspiredWriter/videos

Twitter: https://twitter.com/girlygirlsguide